PRAISE FOR

How to Survive a Bear Attack

Winner of the Governor General's Literary Award for Non-fiction
A *Globe and Mail* Best Book of the Year

"Deeply researched and profoundly moving, Claire Cameron's wonderful book is, at root, a braided love story, by turns heartbreaking and terrifying, but above all brimming with a fierce affection—for her family, for her subjects, and for the precious, precarious act of staying alive. I could not put it down."

—John Vaillant, author of *Fire Weather* and *The Tiger*

"At once a memoir, a meticulously researched investigation, and a meditation on the force of nature, Claire Cameron weaves the narrative together seamlessly in a tale of courage, determination, and, above all else, love. A remarkable achievement that teaches us not only how to survive, but how to thrive, even when the odds are stacked against you."

—David A. Robertson, author of *The Theory of Crows* and *Black Water*

"In a masterful fusion of forensic journalism, nature reporting and memoir, Claire Cameron's account of a deadly incident explores mortality and the consciousness of the wild. *How to Survive a Bear Attack* paddles readers through Algonquin Park rivers and into the halls of medicine, asking them to be brave and inquisitive in order to survive the unexpected."

—Governor General's Literary Awards Jury Citation

"Stunning . . . nature writing at its finest. At its heart, *How to Survive a Bear Attack* is an unforgettable story about finding the courage to face even the wildest of natures within and around us all."

—*Winnipeg Free Press*

"This powerful book asks how we can reconcile the inherent beauty and catharsis of nature with its omnificent, sometimes-frightening power. Readers are offered a moving contemplation of wilderness, survival, and the dangers that lurk unseen within and outside ourselves. The narrative also serves as a compassionate and heartbreaking portrait of an iconic Canadian species." —*NUVO Magazine*

"A brave book." —*Literary Review of Canada*

"If you're drawn to memoirs that explore resilience, the human connection to nature, and the struggle to reconcile past trauma with the present, *How to Survive a Bear Attack* is a must-read. This memoir is a very personal journey of grief, survival, and obsession. What makes it especially compelling is Cameron's ability to weave together themes of survival—both personal and in the face of nature's unpredictability. . . . This memoir is for anyone who enjoys deeply human stories that are raw, honest, and ultimately hopeful."

—*St. Albert Gazette*

PRAISE FOR

The Last Neanderthal

National Bestseller

Finalist for the 2017 Rogers Writers' Trust Fiction Prize

"With great sophistication, *The Last Neanderthal* seeks out that which makes us human and the result is feminist literature of the highest order." —2017 Rogers Writers' Trust Fiction Prize jury

"Deeply sympathetic. . . . [A] vivid survival story."

—*The New York Times*

"Cameron has an exceptional ability to build tension and suspense through tuning us into the drama and plot lines inherent in the natural world. . . . *The Last Neanderthal* masterfully examines our connections to our evolutionary cousins . . . [which] speaks to the author's deep empathy, consummate skill as an artist, and deep-hearted vision. . . . A novel to cherish." —*Toronto Star*

"A powerful, warm, and thought-provoking book that artfully blends facts with fiction to put flesh on many abstract scientific debates." —Yuval Noah Harari, author of *Sapiens* and *Homo Deus*

"A necessary, brilliantly feminist, and intuitive reading of our earliest history. [Cameron] memorably paints a full world with her Neanderthals and binds it perfectly to our own."

—Sheila Heti, author of *Motherhood* and *Alphabetical Diaries*

PRAISE FOR
The Bear

National Bestseller

Longlisted for the Baileys Women's Prize for Fiction

"A gripping survival thriller. . . . This expertly crafted novel could do for camping what *Jaws* did for swimming." —*People*

"Anna's a character who stays with you long after you've put the book down. . . . This is a thrilling and utterly captivating tale."

—*Chatelaine*

"Taut and engrossing. . . . Cameron proves masterly in the creation of a child's fractured worldview. . . . A novel destined to stay with you long after you've chewed through it." —*The Globe and Mail*

"A beautiful novel that is ultimately about maternal love. . . . It made me cry and I couldn't stop."

—Miriam Toews, author of *Women Talking* and *A Truce That Is Not Peace*

"An emotional tour de force. *The Bear* offers us an unforgettable child narrator who propels us through a story as unsettling as it is bone-chilling, and as suspenseful as it is moving."

—Megan Abbott, author of *Dare Me* and *The End of Everything*

HOW TO SURVIVE A BEAR ATTACK

ALSO BY CLAIRE CAMERON

The Line Painter
The Bear
The Last Neanderthal

HOW TO SURVIVE A BEAR ATTACK

A Memoir

CLAIRE CAMERON

Vintage Canada

PUBLISHED IN 2026 BY VINTAGE CANADA
Originally published in hardcover in 2025 by Alfred A. Knopf Canada

Vintage Canada
Penguin Random House Canada Limited
320 Front Street West, Suite 1400
Toronto, Ontario, M5V 3B6, Canada
penguinrandomhouse.ca

The authorized representative in the EU for product safety and compliance is Penguin Random House Ireland, Morrison Chambers, 32 Nassau Street, Dublin D02 YH68, Ireland. https://eu-contact.penguin.ie

LIBRARY AND ARCHIVES CANADA CATALOGUING IN PUBLICATION
Title: How to survive a bear attack : a memoir / Claire Cameron.
Names: Cameron, Claire, 1973- author.
Identifiers: Canadiana 20240391144 | ISBN 9781039056374 (softcover)
Subjects: LCSH: Cameron, Claire, 1973- | LCSH: Bear attacks—Ontario—Algonquin Provincial Park—Case studies. | LCSH: Authors, Canadian—21st century—Biography. | CSH: Authors, Canadian (English)—21st century—Biography. | LCSH: Skin—Cancer—Patients—Canada—Biography. | LCGFT: Autobiographies. LCGFT: Case studies.
Classification: LCC QL737.C27 C36 2026 | DDC 599.7809713/147—dc23

Text and cover design by Emma Dolan
Image credits: *Looking upon the River* by Julie Hart Beers. Original public domain image from Art Institute of Chicago.
Typeset by Erin Cooper

Printed in Canada

2 4 6 8 9 7 5 3 1

Noli timere

—*"Don't be afraid"*
The last message poet Seamus Heaney
sent to his wife, by text, before he died

CONTENTS

HOW TO SURVIVE A BEAR ATTACK

Part One

FIGHT FOR YOUR LIFE

1.

I DON'T BELIEVE IN ghosts, but the campsite where we stood felt heavy with loss. I glanced between the trees, the branches swayed, and a breeze whispered across my cheek. I had come to this remote island by boat with Jerry Schmanda, who had been a member of a search party twenty-eight years before. He stamped a steel-toe rubber boot into the dirt and dragged it. The pine needles parted to either side of his foot to expose the earth underneath. This was what he wanted to show me, a drag mark made by the impression of a body.

We were in a vast wilderness area north of Toronto called Algonquin Park. The browned needles of evergreens lay thick at that time of year. They crunched underfoot. It was early fall and soon the reds, oranges, and yellows would bloom into a riot of colour.

Not yet, though. Before the leaves turn, mid-September, there were still hints of a softer season in the land. Sunlight dappled through the trees, water lapped at a thin strip of beach, and the scent of pine hung heavy in the air. Above us, a raven caught a plume and dipped a wing to slice through the sky.

Terror had ripped through this beautiful place.

Jerry put a hand to his chest and shivered. It happened in 1991, but at that moment, the memory came forward to join us.

"You okay?" I asked.

"It's kind of like the blood moves," he said, describing the surge in his chest. He took a deep breath.

Jerry is fit, lithe, in his fifties, and spry, a body in constant motion. We had only met an hour before, but it felt like longer. He told me about the five winter months he had lived in a cabin in Algonquin Park with four dogs, without a furnace or running water, which he spent chopping firewood endlessly. I could think of nothing better. We had both spent a lot of time in the park. A friendship can be forged by a place.

Algonquin Park is nearly 3,000 square miles, a forest with more than 2,400 lakes and rivers and streams running through it. The borders of the park ring an area the size of Cyprus or Puerto Rico, or about half of New Jersey.

We stood in the middle of the south arm of a large lake called Opeongo. Jerry had brought me here by boat to tell his part of the story. A couple from Toronto went on a camping trip for a long weekend. When they didn't show up for work on Tuesday, their family and friends called the park office. By the time the search party found them, the couple had been missing for five days.

When Jerry pulled up at the campsite in 1991, it looked as if the couple had just arrived. There were paper bags of groceries left in the boat. The Coleman stove had been lit and gone cold. A tent was set up. There were two camping chairs by the ring of rocks that marked the fire, one chair knocked over, one still upright. A Styrofoam tray of ground beef sat by the fire. It was untouched except for a tiny prick in the plastic. "Like a raven had picked at it or something," Jerry said.

The search party climbed out of the boats and spread out to do a hasty search, a quick look around for any sign of life. They talked quietly among themselves as they did. None of them knew what to make of what they saw. They speculated about things like suicide, double suicide, or murder-suicide—all guesses far more statistically likely than the reality. This was a crime scene of a different kind.

One of the searchers wondered aloud if the couple had been hurt. If either one or both had tried to make it back by land, they would have crossed the water via a short channel. From there, they might have had to climb a hill, but even if disoriented or lost, they would sooner or later run into a road. With hindsight, Jerry said, "It didn't make sense—that would be a day or two." They would have been found already.

Jerry showed me where he'd opened the flap of the tent. He remembered a thin inflatable camping mattress inside with a dusty paw print on it. He didn't think much of it at the time. With food left around and no people at the site, animals were bound to come through. The sleeping bags were still wrapped up in plastic garbage bags. It looked as though the couple hadn't even spent the night.

We walked up the slight slope toward the back of the campsite. The land climbs toward a ridge that runs the length of the island like a backbone. There the underbrush is thicker with balsams, small spruce, and shrubs. It provides cover. If I crouched down, it would be difficult for someone standing by the campfire to spot me.

Jerry pointed to where the bodies were found. "My dad was a butcher," he said, explaining why he went to look at them. His fingers didn't touch me, but he mimed the action of a slice on my shoulder. "The flesh peeled off the bone. You could see the shoulder. A fully intact hand."

I had only told Jerry part of my story. He didn't know he was tracing a large scar still raw from the deep cut made ten months earlier. I had three other scars—one at the side of my ribs, another at the small of my back, and a short gash at the base of my neck. The wounds were healed but still sensitive to heat and cold and touch. I tried not to flinch.

When the men in the search party found the drag marks, they knew something had gone terribly wrong. Staying close, they walked level with each other in a line to follow the marks up the slope toward the back of the campsite.

Jerry and I retraced their steps.

At first, the trees were spread wide apart and it was easy to walk between them. Mixed in between the sturdy pines were a few birch trees with silvery bark that had been peeled back. The dirt was packed tight around the base of the trees. Their roots wove through the ground like veins under skin. A gentle breeze pushed the canopy back and forth in a sway like it was breathing.

The men had kept moving in the line toward the denser bush at the back of the campsite. An officer with the Ontario Provincial Police, Steve Swrjeski, heard a sound. He told everyone to stand still. They listened. Again they heard a huff, a kind of cough.

There was something on the island with them. It took cover

in the brush. It was watching and knew they were approaching. The huff was a warning: they shouldn't come any closer.

"So then"—Jerry pointed up to where the sound came from, his hand touching his chest again—"we said, bear."

2.

I WENT TO THE island with Jerry as part of an investigation. In 1991, a black bear had killed two adults in a rare predatory attack. I wanted to understand what happened. I wanted to understand why.

I had first heard of the bear attack in October of that same year. It made the front page of the newspaper. The headline caught my attention, as I planned to work in Algonquin Park the next summer. The details about the attack were sparse. After reading the article, I had more questions than answers.

For thirty-plus years since, I've continued to ask what happened in Algonquin Park.

Sometimes, I've asked with a purpose in mind. I've gone on missions to try to understand the attack at different times in my life. For a while, I searched in creative work. I wrote a novel, *The Bear*, that pivoted around some facts and distorted others. I hoped that if I could set my fears down on paper, I could write them away.

Other times, I've asked what happened on that island in my sleep. I've woken in a sweat, breathing heavily and in distress. In this recurring dream, either I am running or I've fallen on the ground. I can't get up. The sun is shining in my eyes; it is hard to see, and a dark shape shifts just out of view. I hear a huff and wake. Only then do I understand—a predatory bear is hiding in my dreams.

A few years ago, I became obsessed with this bear attack again. I knew it was an incredibly rare event, but still, the attack continued to haunt me. Deciding I'd let my imagination run wild, I went looking for answers grounded in science. I launched a formal investigation into the black bear attack in Algonquin Park.

There's a box in my office that overflows with manila folders, photocopies with highlighted text, and binder clips. It's stuffed with papers I collected after filing freedom of information requests with the government, visiting archives, and finding dusty articles printed on yellowed paper. There are books with highlighted passages and lined articles from academic journals. I have transcriptions from interviews with people who were in the search party, police officers, and wildlife biologists. I have notes from conversations with academics, including one of the foremost experts on bear attacks, Dr. Stephen Herrero. I interviewed the victims' families and friends, and bear attack survivors. All these sources have informed this story.

If a bear attack is sensational enough, the first stories in the media may go viral. Often, these stories are full of confusion and half-digested facts. This is for good reason. It is difficult to report in a wilderness setting, and often journalists are working remotely. Experts wait to comment until they have more complete information. Those who will talk often have only part of the story.

After initial reports, sometimes there are thorough investigations into bear attacks, but the results are rarely printed. They don't go viral. The expert opinions, given after careful consideration and weighing of the evidence, won't make the front page or be shared on social media. The findings can be hard to access or aren't made public.

Some books and articles about bear attacks are gory and lurid. Others take an overly sentimental view of bears, or skip a discussion of attacks altogether. Many films leave science behind and turn bears into monsters hell-bent on revenge. Bears are used as logos for sports teams, as children's toys, and to sell cookies. Bears are loved, worshipped, hated, killed, saved, or treated like a nuisance.

What happened in Algonquin Park, two adults killed by a black bear, is so rare that it can be seen as a statistical anomaly. In the last twenty years, just over one person per year has been killed by a black bear in North America. By focusing people's attention on attacks, I worry that I will add to the mischaracterization of bear behaviour in the public perception. Sharks, tigers, snakes, and wolves—when large predators are positioned as the enemy of humans, they have been killed in the thousands. Sometimes to the edge of extinction.

While getting to know the people connected with this attack, including a wider circle of family members and friends, I came to understand that their experiences are not anomalies. When the value of a life is taken into account, and a large dose of love is added, statistics become drained of their meaning. Life is all or nothing.

Between these points lies my obsession. I love bears. I've studied them for more than twenty-five years, and have had many uneventful encounters with them, so why my bloodthirsty focus?

I grew up with the idea that the wilderness and the city are separate from each other. The false border I drew between them helped hold my fear in place.

My investigation follows three main lines of inquiry. The bear is the most important. This took me years to understand, but it was his decision that changed everything that came after. The couple are also important, as are the people who were in the search party, but they are only part of this story because they were in a certain place at a specific time.

I am the third line of inquiry. I wasn't directly involved in what happened, but my interest has been led by personal circumstances. To understand the events of that evening in October 1991, I had to uncover the obsessive forces behind my questions. They drove the investigation.

"The past is a foreign country. They do things differently there" reads the first line of *The Go-Between* by L.P. Hartley. It's a wrenchingly beautiful way to acknowledge the inaccessibility of all that has come before. The past hovers in the distance, prone to blurring. Some accounts are unreliable, many witnesses are lost, all versions of a story become intangible. An investigation is an attempt to do the impossible, to reach out and touch and describe how it felt, the taste, the smell. But the past is a land we can't visit anymore. I can't bring it back, but I can try to tell a complete story. It's a way of passing on the feeling of standing somewhere we can no longer be.

After years of investigation, I've come to understand that behind my obsession with this specific incident lay a question: If I'm attacked by a bear, will I survive? At its heart, this book tells the story of how I found the answer.

3.

MY BATTLE STARTED EARLY. I remember the last words my dad spoke to me.

I was nine years old when I was called to his bedroom. He lay propped on a pillow. I crawled onto the bed to lie beside him, careful not to jostle, knowing he was fragile. He wore the large glasses of a bookish man. They often slipped down his nose, but by then he was so thin they barely stayed on.

When he looked at me, I was surprised to see tears in his eyes.

"I'm going to die," he said.

I didn't react. Instead, I stared at the ceiling and noticed a crack in the plaster. I was too young to know what to say. Should I cry?

His cancer started as melanoma, the deadliest skin cancer, and then it spread. I remember an operation, a large bite with metal staples like teeth that ran up his side. I remember chemotherapy as a nuclear event that wasted his body. In life, he stood six feet five inches tall. By the end, he touched down close to a hundred pounds.

My dad, Angus, was much more than cancer. He grew up in Truro, Nova Scotia, read a row of encyclopedias from A to Z, played pickup baseball, and left the Maritimes to study at Oxford University. He had a rolling sense of humour, loved opera, and quietly pined for a two-seater sports car, the kind his legs were too long to fold into. He became a professor at the University of Toronto. He founded *The Dictionary of Old English*.

He was a loving husband, brother, and father who told me bedtime stories. The story I loved the most was his version of *Beowulf*, an epic poem and one of the earliest written examples of Old English, dated from around AD 1000. It tells the story of a hero, Beowulf, who fights three monsters, each one more terrifying than the one who came before. First comes Grendel, a flesh-eating beast; next is his wicked mother, bent on vengeance; and the last battle is against a night-flying dragon who terrorizes the land.

My dad's retelling of *Beowulf* had everything: shining swords, brave acts, fierce battles, and gold cups. I loved Grendel the most. He was an outcast prone to bouts of jealous rage. In their first battle, Beowulf ripped off Grendel's arm and pinned it above the door in the mead hall. Grendel's mother had to go and get it back for him.

My dad explained the idea of a kenning in *Beowulf*, a description that stands for a noun.

"*Whale-road*," he said. "Can you guess what that is?"

It means ocean. Immediately, I understood the magic in kennings. *Whale* and *road*—the two words are not like each other, but if you are willing to let one lend meaning to the other, a new relationship is unlocked. They can shift my perspective. When I put them together, I become a whale gliding through the water in a channel. The two words become less like a label and more like an orientation—a new way of seeing.

A bracelet is an *arm-serpent*. Fire is *wind's brother*. The chest is the *thought-land*. An eye is an *eyelash-moon*. A bear is a *greedy-tooth*.

Beowulf had a special sword. This weapon was so powerful that it had a name, Hrunting. To my young mind, the name meant the blade had a personality. It was a sentient being that helped me win battles. With a tangle of messy hair and drooping pyjamas, I fought alongside my dad's story with my imaginary sword held high. The fire-breathing dragon was the most fearsome, a monster that posed an existential threat to the people. It flew around at night and burned all the houses down. I stood tall on the mattress, held the weapon up to the sky, and roared.

By the end of my dad's story, the green body of the dragon, embodied by my pillow, lay on the mattress between us. I twisted my sword and finished him off. We both waited, watching, until the pillow stopped twitching.

"Is it dead?" I asked.

"At least it was quick," my dad said.

But my dad's death wasn't quick. It was slow. Cancer spread to his lymph nodes. My dad started slipping. He became less lucid and needed more sedation. His eyebrows were gone. His thick brown curls fell out and thin wisps took their place. They were light and fluffy and barely covered his head. Rather than the death of cells, I saw the progress of his disease more like a regression. No hair, big blue eyes, his frame shrinking. The man who continues to melt back to the size of a child might one day become a baby. Back from where he came.

My dad's *day-count* fell short. He died on May 27, 1983. He was forty-two years old.

IF YOUR DAD DIES and you are in grade four, you don't have to go to school that day. Or the day after. At first, it was like a strange holiday. I was allowed to watch too much TV. No one monitored my plate to see if I'd finished my peas. I was home for about a week.

When I went back to school, it felt like a sombre birthday party. The kids crowded around me in silence when I entered the classroom. Some of them gave me cards. A girl my age, Julie, was the only one to say something out loud. She stood in front of me with folded hands and gave a slight bow. "I'm very sorry about your dad." At the time, this seemed formal and kind. Now, it is even more touching as I imagine the coaching her parents probably did to prepare her in advance.

Everywhere I went, friends and neighbours touched my hair, gave me an extra cookie, or told me I was strong and brave. My friend's mom traced the dark circle under my eye. Maybe she wondered why I wasn't crying, but she didn't ask. This was a silent gesture, a kindness. I didn't have the words to describe the weather inside.

Life went on and it seemed fine, except it wasn't.

I had bangs. I didn't want them. My hair was thick, blond, and hard to tame, where I wished it was more like Princess Leia's, impossibly shiny, brown, in two neat buns.

The other girls started wearing these short, folded socks with a little frill around the top. I didn't have money of my own to buy them and I didn't want to ask my mom. She was knee-deep in insurance claims and frozen accounts. The university where my dad had been employed was going through a miserly patch. She was ensnared in a series of administrative tasks that stretched her thin. Those first years were incredibly hard for my mom, I knew that much. My way of observing her suffering was to hold myself in what felt like an equally difficult position—I didn't ask for money to buy the frilly socks.

Quietly, my bangs went about ruining everything.

I was angry. I had tantrums. Everyone knew why. Everyone except me.

Grief can overwhelm. My young body shut down. And then, at some point, I went numb. I stopped feeling sad. When my sister cried, I felt sorry that she was sad. On some level, I couldn't understand why she would bother crying. It wouldn't change anything. My dad was dead. Tears weren't going to bring him back.

My grandmother magically transported herself from Montreal into our living room. She didn't drive and must have taken the train. Usually when she visited, we went to pick her up. I loved making the trip to Union Station, with its marbled pillars, broad stone, and red-cap porters.

This time, though, my grandmother simply appeared in our house. She was Gran. Once, I called her Granny and she looked down her nose. "Are you trying to make me sound old?" She had tidy ankles, always crossed. She wore cashmere sweaters, houndstooth skirts, and a string of pearls; her hair was set in a stand-up dryer during a weekly appointment. Her leather pumps were polished, with a square heel. They matched her purse. That day, she sat with a cigarette in hand and a crystal tumbler with brown liquid two fingers deep. She smoked Vantage Lights. The reduced nicotine was a concession, the downgrade to show she was behaving after a warning from her doctor. She pulled her thumb along the lighter, a Bic.

As a dedicated smoker, the elegant kind, Gran often looked as though she was on a movie set. She would dangle a cigarette from two fingers and talk, and people would always start laughing. The tip of her ring finger pressed lightly against the pad of her thumb.

This cigarette, however, was swaying with her trembling hand. I put my hand on her leg, and it was only then I realized she was crying. Softly, a lone tear made its way through the light press of powder toward her lipstick mouth.

"Darn this thing," she said. Her thumb pulled along the dial of the lighter once more, a grind of flint, and a flame jumped up. She touched it to the tip of her cigarette. We were both relieved to hear the crackle of paper and tobacco pulling back from the ember. She let a breath out and immediately seemed better.

"Can I have one?" I asked.

"Pardon?"

"A cigarette," I said, thinking it worth a try, as everything else in my life had changed beyond recognition.

"If your poor mother came in to find us smoking?" She put a hand on my arm and laughed softly. "We'd kill her too."

Together, we decided not to kill my mother. I sat with Gran while she smoked for both of us.

I did my best to grow my bangs. They only moved as far as my eyes and then seemed to get stuck. Half blinded by a thick shelf of blond hair, I tried to keep going.

In that first year after my dad died, I reversed the decision that I was too old for my doll, Daisy. She took up her second life beside me. She had eyes that blinked shut when I moved her head. Her lashes were long. When I tried to have a conversation with her, she gave me a blank stare. The blue of her painted irises seemed dead, almost creepy. Something had changed between us. There was no going back to how we were before.

Part Two

BE PREPARED

4.

HEALING, WHEN IT CAME, took on the shape of adventure. I discovered a love sharp enough to pierce my armour in the form of travelling by canoe. A few years after my father's death, I went on a wilderness course with a company called Outward Bound. We did a long canoe trip along the White River, which feeds into Lake Superior. On the day we reached the lake, so large it's an inland sea, we had to wait for calm. Finally, we paddled out on rolling waves that were long and broad. The boat beside mine dipped to disappear in a trough. When the water rose again, our companions in the same boat appeared overhead.

The water in Superior changed something inside me. The clouds loosened. They broke. The waves flattened and smoothed as we made our way along the shoreline. I understood the power in a body of water, how much influence it had over everything around us. I resolved to get myself back into a canoe whenever I could.

I still missed my dad. My grief could be sharp, but the wilderness held so many ways to divert my attention. Surrounded by friends, I kept going out in canoes, on foot, and started scaling rocks. I plunged into the blue water, sat under a wide sky, and travelled in the company of trees. I spent my best days exposed to the elements in blistering sun, downpours, and surprise hailstorms. I swatted mosquitoes, ran rapids, and portaged between the lakes on winding trails. My hair now a tangled braid hanging down my back, those bangs were finally in my past. I paddled for miles.

Deep into bear country I went.

IN JULY 1992, I went to live and work in Algonquin Park at a summer camp. I was nineteen years old. Growing up in the city, in Toronto, meant I wanted to leave the smog, cement, crowds, and fumes whenever possible. Most people in Canada live along the southern border. Heading north set a direction for my imagination. By then I was strong from all the activity, limbs browned and long hair bleached by the sun.

I took a cabin of eleven-year-old girls out on a ten-day canoe trip through the backcountry. I remember how the sharp smell of pine was released when crushed by a soggy sneaker, the line of trees on the shore sliding beside the canoe, a lake flat like glass. My fingers were often sticky from marshmallow residue or sap. To keep our bags light we wore the same dirty T-shirts the whole trip, the shredded grey cotton worn like a badge of honour. We paddled for miles every day.

The feeling of being perfectly in sync with a small group of people overtook us on that trip. These girls were young, but fast and strong. We travelled at around three miles an hour on water and took the sections on land at a similar speed. We'd nose up to a portage and spring into action. Each of the three staff would take a pack and lift a canoe onto our shoulders. Each camper had a set task, the tallest taking the heavy box with kitchen supplies, and whoever had the most blisters that day would take a lighter armful of life jackets and paddles. Depending on the terrain, we covered around twenty miles a day. Our muscles were power, food became fuel, and our progress in life could be traced with a grubby finger on a map.

At the end of the day the colours broke across the sky, yellow, gold, then red, they seeped into purple and spread out to show us why it was worth having messy braids and wet socks. The night swallowed us up. A sound sleep, worn muscles, and dry feet—these become the greatest luxuries.

One day, we were travelling through the eastern side of the park. The land sits lower; there are more cedars and swamps. We carried our packs, boats, paddles, and gear over a long portage. At what looked like the end, the six preteen girls were exhausted and collapsed on the soft gear bags. We still had to repack the canoes, paddle across a long lake, and then find the campsite. Seeing the group energy lacking, I broke out the cookies.

The water was high. It had been raining non-stop. At the end of the portage, the path dipped into the water and turned into mud. This particular kind of mud had a name: moose muck. Moose could often be found standing in it, chewing on plants. They have long legs for wading through the sticky mess. On a person, the same mud would be waist or chest deep. Aside from the occasional mud fight, we tried to stay out of moose muck at all costs.

There were two staff members with me, a guide and a counsellor in training. The guide was well-meaning, charming, and often stunned by the obstacles life put in front of him. His face tilted to the sun, eyes closed, a long piece of grass sticking out of his mouth.

"Is this the end of the portage?" I asked.

The guide rubbed his stubble and squinted at the map. It was drawn for canoe routes at a scale of 1:126,720, or two miles to the inch. Every map shrinks the terrain down to a manageable size. In doing so, details are lost. Small cliffs, coves, or bends in a trail don't always show up. It was easy enough to adjust the eye for this. We relied on bigger features, like a point of land, an island, or the shape of a lake. From there, it was possible to extrapolate how the land would behave.

"We're in the crease," the guide said.

He had folded the map a few times to fit, facing out, in a zip-lock bag. At some point, the bag had taken on moisture. The red line that traced our way had been rubbed away. The worn crease left behind was about half an inch wide and fell directly over our route.

We were left to find our way without the map. We spent the next hour looking through the bush, but came to cliffs and dense brush. We had to go through the mud.

The next three hours were epic. I spent most of them in warm mud that sometimes went up to my armpits. It was too deep for the girls, so we put them in the canoes, two at a time, and dragged the boat over top. It's possible to become accustomed to the stench of moose muck. The smell of rotten eggs, a gassy belch, and old feces mixed together didn't bother me after a while. The things I liked less were strange creatures touching my bare skin in the depths. I felt teeth in my knee. It may have been a stick, but I'll never know because I couldn't see into the water more than a few inches. I started picking off leeches, no big deal, and flicking them away.

Several times, I tripped and fell face-first. I picked myself up and saw two eyes peering over the edge of the canoe. It was one of the campers, who wondered if, after falling, I would disappear into the brown goo forever.

She tried to make me smile. "Maybe it's good for your skin?"

We found a dry point of land with clear water on the other side. When we reached the campsite, it was with a sense of victory. We had made it to the edge of the crease. In the morning, our route turned back beyond the fold. Everyone went swimming to clean off. We laid our clothes around the rocks to dry. The girls told us to sit while they made dinner.

Something took root inside me that day; an idea was planted. Life could be unpredictable. I didn't necessarily ask to wallow in the mud. Once there, though, I was fine. I could be kind. I could be strong. I could help to keep the people around me safe. That summer filled me with a feeling of power.

In Algonquin Park, I found myself.

ON THE NEXT CANOE trip I led that summer, we put the boats into Opeongo Lake. It's the largest lake in the park. I was worried about the wind. Opeongo yawns out wide from the shore on either side. The headwinds can be soul-destroying. As boats go, canoes are efficient to paddle because they are narrow and slice through the water. But this also leaves their broadsides vulnerable to getting lapped by water.

I made sure all three boats stayed close to the shore, and we paddled hard. About a half-hour into the journey, we turned around the bend, hugging the shoreline to the east.

I saw a name on the map: Bates Island. It had made the front page of a newspaper the year before because of the bear attack. The island was named after a trapper who had lived on the lake, but it stuck in my mind because of Alfred Hitchcock's famous psychopath, Norman Bates. Everything in the article had come as a shock. I didn't know a black bear could attack two adults and kill them. It had sounded like the plot of a horror movie, not reality.

Up to that moment, I had thought of black bears as overgrown raccoons. You had to be careful of the garbage or they would make a mess, they licked greasy barbecue grills, and it wasn't a good idea to corner a bear. I knew a mother grizzly with cubs could pose a threat, but most of the time, when I saw a black bear, I clapped. The bear ran off.

Seeing the island on the map made me uneasy. I selected a campsite to get some distance between our tents and the island. When our day was finally done, the girls were sleeping soundly in the tent. I built up the fire, kept my back to the water, and peered into the woods.

The guide I was working with for that trip, Louis, sat down beside me. We stared at the flames as they devoured the logs. He told me what he'd heard about the attack. A Styrofoam tray of ground beef had been found at the campsite. A broken paddle had been lying near the water. He leaned closer and whispered, "It ate them."

That night in my tent, I tried to fill in the gaps. What else did I not know? I was camped on the same lake, near the same island, and used similar equipment. I could imagine every moment that led up to the attack, but nothing after: the sights, the sounds, the smells. The details started to haunt me. They circled the tent. They crept into my dreams.

The next day, I woke up early and crawled out of my sleeping bag. On some mornings in Algonquin, the lake is completely still and calm. The water holds a perfect tension. Alone, before everyone else was up, I sat by the lake, its reflection a mirror. The world split in two, one up top and a replica below. They both looked true.

Soon, the air warmed just enough to tip the balance. The slightest breeze appeared across the surface of the water, rippling, and time took hold of the lake again. The day broke through.

It would take me more than thirty years to understand the fight that had taken place on the lake.

5.

THE COUPLE, RAY AND Carola, left the city on Friday, October 10, 1991. Though they didn't know it, their battle started on the drive from Toronto to Algonquin Park.

Their car slid through the west end of the city, past concrete blocks, shimmering glass, the tangle of bodies, the sirens and machines. The population of Toronto has almost doubled since 1991, but the route most people take to Algonquin Park is still the same. They stayed on city streets until they found their way on the highway west to merge onto Highway 400, the main road that heads north.

Once on the highway, the car broke loose and sped up. Around it, the slabs of pavement narrowed. The stretches of dirt, grass, and trees started to reach wider. Gas stations and exits became less frequent. Green sprung up outside the window, maples, oaks, a stand of poplars. There were dogwood and cedar and cattails in the ditches. The farmers' fields grew longer and broader.

Soon the horizon touched down to the ground on either side of the car. Overhead, the sky soared.

This wasn't the couple's first trip to Algonquin Park. His name was Raymond Jakubauskas, or Ray, and he was thirty-two years old. He wore glasses, sensible wire frames, and worked for the postal service. Her name was Carola Frehe and she was forty-eight. She is described by loved ones as a striking, boisterous woman with a German accent. Even the grainy copy of a photo I found in an archive shows her beauty. She was an office administrator. Carola was Ray's first serious girlfriend, according to a childhood friend. "Some people thought the age gap was a bit much," he said. "You could certainly see how much in love they were and I don't think it bothered them a bit."

About an hour and a half or so into the trip, the tips of the trees changed. They became more pointed, leaner. Evergreens, with spiky needles, started to stand in for their broadleaf southern cousins. Pine trees form the backbone of the northern forest, perfectly adapted to hold nutrients through the low light and frigid temperatures of a long winter.

Soon, beside the couple's car, the continental shelf breached the surface of the soil. The rock rose higher and climbed into the sky to take the shape of a cliff. This is part of the Canadian Shield, a massive expanse of granite that stretches from the Great Lakes to the Arctic Ocean. There is so much ore in the Shield that it can affect a magnet from across the continent.

The Shield has incredible strength, but not the kind that stands up to dynamite. As they kept driving, they would have seen the marks from the explosives, cylinder-shaped scars, running the length of the exposed faces of granite. It was blown apart to make room for the new highway to allow a straighter route. The gates forced open; their car sliced through.

In 1991, Highway 400 narrowed into two lanes farther south than it does now. The couple probably turned off at a town called Huntsville to take Highway 60, which bisects the southern end of Algonquin Park. This road was paved in 1948. The main route through the park is along that corridor. It leads the way to trailheads, canoe rental stores, lookouts, and it's where cars pull over to take photos when the people inside spot a moose.

The rivers and streams thread the lakes of Algonquin Park together. In the backcountry, most people travel by canoe. When they hit the end of one waterway, they portage—they turn their canoe onto their shoulders, like a second head, and carry it over a path to get to the next lake, river, or creek. In the summer months, people go on canoe trips for days and weeks and months this way.

The couple had stopped to rent a runabout, a small aluminum boat with an outboard motor on the back, from a rental place called Avery's. This boat was about fourteen feet in length. It was open to the elements and comfortably carried two people and their gear.

Opeongo is one of the few lakes in the park that allows motors. It has a boat ramp and is one of the primary put-ins where commercial tours and water taxis launch.

When they turned left off the highway onto the access road to the interior, the couple were heading into the heart of the wilderness. There are established campsites in Algonquin Park with services like running water, electricity, toilets, and showers, but Ray and Carola went into the backcountry. At that time of year, the middle of October, far fewer people take that route.

Immediately, the road became lonelier. The tires bumped over potholes and they drove slowly; the pavement gets chewed by ice in the winter. If they came up to another car, they had to nudge over to the side to pass it.

At the end of the access road is Algonquin Outfitters. In 1991, Jerry Schmanda worked there. It's a large building made with thick timber that looks like a lodge. It is one of the more popular access points for the backcountry, selling coffee, T-shirts, and key chains with tiny black bears dangling from a link. The store rents out everything you need: canoes, paddles, life jackets, and barrels that make it harder for chipmunks and bears to get at your food. There's an office to buy camping permits.

The couple pulled up and parked their car in the gravel lot.

The staff in the store noted the couple's arrival. Ray came into the outfitting store asking for a plug for the bottom of their boat, which was missing. They lent him one, the store being the kind of place where missing a plug for a boat wouldn't require a transaction.

The couple loaded their gear from their car into the boat. They pushed off from the dock around 5:30 p.m.

Opeongo is 150 feet deep in some places and stretches wide from the shore on either side. The couple had an advantage over my trips in a canoe because they had a small motor to power them. To get to the island wouldn't take more than ten minutes, maybe a little longer if they stopped or slowed to fish.

A large stretch of water cools more slowly than the land around it. The warmer air over the lake can cause a layer of water to evaporate. Some evenings, the mist seems to be rising off the water, obscuring shapes and dampening all sound. Once you're on the water, the spires of the pine trees are the first things to come into view. There might be the wail of a loon, a water bird that looks like an elegant duck dressed in a black-and-white tux. Loons live in pairs and cry to find each other, their searching calls cutting through fog like a haunting, long and mournful.

As the couple drove across the lake, the motor was the dominant sound. The sky must have thickened with dusk as the night closed in. Fingers red and bent clutching the rudder, the couple would need warm coats to pull around their necks as they sped over the water toward the island.

In October there isn't usually snow on the ground yet, but according to historical weather data the temperature had only climbed to ten degrees Celsius that day. There were two millimetres of precipitation, enough for a fine mist, but not much more.

Whether by motorboat or canoe, going into the backcountry in the fall is a bold move. From mid-September until winter ice locks in the lake, travelling there is only for the hardy. It's cold. The clouds turn grey and press down. The wind slaps at cheeks and the water turns steely. Everywhere, there are signs of living things hunkering down, taking shelter, storing, and closing up. It's a time of retreat. If you listen closely, there's a deep pulse to the land, a quickening.

When the couple left the dock, it was the last time anyone saw them alive.

6.

THE BEAR STARTED PREPARING for his battle when he went to sleep in October 1990.

He found a site for a den to spend the winter that wasn't far from Opeongo Lake. The spot was under a large white pine where another bear had lingered before. Giving it a thorough sniff, he identified the other bear. He understood where each paw had been placed, and knew that the other bear hadn't been back for a while. This was a safe spot. He dug a den to make it a perfect size.

When there were no more good prospects for food, the bear crawled in to go to sleep.

A den is as individual as the bear who sleeps inside it. They are sometimes located in small caves, cliffs, or hollowed-out slopes. I've seen them under large trees; the bear must have curled up like a ball of roots. Some dens are dug out; other times, bears make do with naturally occurring shapes. They often have an entrance that gives way to a slightly larger alcove.

Once the bear has tucked away, the den can be hard to spot. A breathing hole might provide the only clue. I've heard more than one story of a biologist trying to track the location of a bear, only to realize they are standing almost on top of the sleeping animal.

Once settled, the bear looked soft and docile. His muscles were rounded and proud. He'd had a good year, which you could see in his coat. It was thick, a glossy black. It shone with health. If you put a palm on his shoulder, the thick hairs would tickle. But if you dug your fingers into his fur, there was an undercoat soft and dense enough to repel water. His winter coat had grown in.

He was a black bear. His fur was black, but he had relatives with lighter coats, almost gingery at the flank, or cinnamon in colour. Some black bears have an arch to their snout, but his nose ran almost flat from the sensitive pad at the tip, between his eyes, and to his ears.

On a human, the eyes tell the direction of a person's attention. On a bear, it's better to follow their ears. His were fuzzy, large, and expressive. They showed his moods.

Those ears fell back. The bear relaxed in his den. His lips went soft. His paws were about five inches across, the size of a man's hand. He curled into a ball for warmth, with a balsam branch beside him.

A black bear goes into a deep sleep during the winter. His body temperature dropped from around thirty-eight to thirty-three degrees Celsius. His heart rate slowed from sixty to ninety beats per minute to eight or ten. He started using about half the energy he would outside the den, but he would only lose fat, not muscle or bone mass. This state is commonly called a hibernation, but it's technically a torpor. The bear could stir if threatened or attacked; he could wake to escape.

In warmer climates, or where food is abundant, some bears don't sleep away the winter. Some might go down for a few days. The length of sleep depends on the climate and the availability of food. It's a survival strategy.

This bear could sleep in his den for a hundred days or longer without eating, drinking, or having to get up and go outside for a pee. What urine his body made was reabsorbed in the bladder. It went through a recycling process and turned into protein used to repair bones and tissue.

The bear was seven and a half years old when he climbed into the den. He turned his nose toward the balsam branch. He pulled one into his den every year for comfort, a habit he had learned from his mother. One sniff would bring a memory as a sensation in his nose. The branch held a reminder of his long life outside, the scent a reminder of the warm sun and longer days with plenty to eat. In the wild, some black bears live about ten years, but they can live up to twenty-five years, and the oldest known black bear died after living for thirty-nine and a half years.

In mid-April, the bear turned in the tight space. He noticed changes outside, a difference in how the air stirred around him. The winds stopped howling. He yawned, he stretched, he cracked open one eye, gummy and thick with sleepy crust, but he quickly closed it.

A day later, he woke again. His head wanted to sleep, but the scents of spring found his nose. The balsam branch brushed against it. His stomach grumbled. Hunger was the only thing strong enough to rouse him.

A wildlife biologist named Jeremy Inglis studied large male black bears in Algonquin Park with his partner, Mike Wilton.

They started their work in 1992, the year after the Bates Island attack. Before their study, most research on black bears focused on mothers and cubs, to learn more about the breeding population. The study of large males provided new insights. "To understand a bear," Inglis told me, "get to know his stomach."

When the bear lumbered out of his den, he was drowsy, legs shaky, and the pads of his paws were sensitive to the brittle land around him. Snow was still on the ground in patches. Around that time, the ice had moved out from the water. Aside from the ice breakup of the lake, there was little other movement. Only the squirrels were rustling, and many birds were still gone, but the first buds on the ends of a few branches were pressing to get out.

The bear stayed near his den for the first few weeks, a smaller area where he knew what food he could find. Wandering too far felt unnecessarily risky while he was still waking up after a long winter nap.

On the ground, he found some nuts from the previous season. He drank from a stream. He chewed on grasses, but the portion was meagre. His belly continued to growl and became increasingly demanding. Spring, then or now, is a precarious time for a bear. He had lost 25 to 40 percent of his body fat during the winter, and the land was not yet providing.

It is hard work to feed the body of a large mammal off the land. It takes skill, persistence, and grit, but this bear was good at solving problems.

Male black bears generally weigh between 160 and 220 pounds. The males are larger than females by about 30 percent. They stand around three feet high at the shoulder. A man from Longlac in Ontario killed a black bear weighing 760 pounds.

This bear was not that large, but he was big. When he died, he weighed close to 310 pounds. He lived for eight and a half years, around the age when they tend to reach their maximum height and weight. This was his prime.

The necropsy, a post-mortem examination of an animal, found the bear in good condition. His teeth were healthy. He had fat deposits around the base of his spine and rump that were at least two inches thick. The bone marrow in his femur, a measure of condition as it's the last fat reserve the body will use, appeared healthy. He had a neck that measured twenty-nine inches, about the same circumference as one of Dwayne "The Rock" Johnson's thighs.

THAT SPRING, FOOD WAS scarce, but the bear was resourceful. A forest, like the one found in Algonquin Park, was his natural habitat. His black coat gave him protection. He blended in, slipping between the trees and hiding in the shadows.

The bear lived mostly on plants. Depending on their habitat, vegetation might make up 85 percent of a black bear's diet. They have long intestines, which are able to absorb cellulose, the structural component in plants. About 25 million years ago, the carnassial teeth, the shearing teeth, flattened to allow for the crushing and chewing of plants.

He was always curious about novel kinds of food when he came across them. Stumps were overturned and pawed into pieces. He dug for insects and larvae in rotten wood. He waded into eddies in the rivers and checked under rocks. He climbed a tree to see if any fruit had managed to hang on. The first green shoots, flowers, leaves, and buds are important as they are easy to digest and nutritious.

The bear travelled in an area about eighty-seven square miles in size. It was a range, not a set territory. He revisited the places that had sources of food he'd eaten before. First he'd travelled with his mother, and then on his own. He had retraced his movements for eight years by then.

Every year, as the bear roamed, he grew bigger. If the chances he took for food paid off, he might grow larger and bolder with every year after that. He lived every day to eat and doze and then wake to eat again in preparation for what was coming.

He mostly scavenged and foraged, but he craved protein because it added bulk to his muscles like nothing else could. He always had an eye out for meat. If he found the chance, he would hunt.

Part Three

SECURE YOUR FOOD

7.

AS MY LOVE OF the wilderness grew, my tolerance for risk became steeper.

I travelled west and found the terrain of the mountains. I started climbing. I stood at the top of rocky peaks, paddled boiling rivers, and became tougher by travelling through the desert. I hiked through the high scrub to a glacier on Mount Hood in Oregon. As part of a rescue training exercise to become a guide, I tied my harness onto a rope, walked backwards off the gleaming ice and over the lip of a crevasse.

About thirty feet down, in the belly of the glacier, I found a place more spectacular than any cathedral. The slick of ice was carved and twisted. It turned bright turquoise and dove into black. As I hung on the rope, I knew the glacier was alive around me, groaning, gurgling, and cracking. The ice was ancient, and in comparison, the span of human life seemed inconsequential. I started to come to terms with the death of my dad. Grief doesn't just go; it changes shape and grows. Mine found its scale.

To fund my climbing habit, I started planting trees. I was in university by then, and during the spring I could work as a tree planter for two months and then take the summer off to go climbing out west. That was my idea of rich: enough money for gas and a climbing rope.

I lived alongside many black bears near Hearst, Ontario, halfway between Toronto and James Bay. The days were long. The trees were shorter than I'd seen before because of the compact growing season in the north. The ice let go around the time of our arrival, in early May.

We worked in clear-cuts where trees had been previously harvested. At first glance, all that was left behind was scrub, brush, mud, and devastation. The land had been logged and slashed and burned. But after a year, there were often signs of regeneration. In the ash, the life that managed to hang on had a good chance, the green shoots pushing through the burn, birds nesting, and more bugs than I'd ever imagined could possibly exist.

I usually made between nine and eleven cents for each tree I planted, depending on the contract. At my peak, I planted about four thousand a day. They were mostly black spruce, scrubby seedlings with long tails of wet roots.

In the early season, my steel-toe boots would break through shallow puddles covered with a translucent film of ice. I had duct tape wrapped around each finger and both heels to cover up the blisters. I wore a bandana on my head and ripped shirts. When I wiped the sweat off my face, I left dirt on my lip in the shape of a handlebar moustache. I had three bags of trees, one on each hip and one in the back. My job was to plant them. That was it. Take two steps, grab a tree with one hand while clearing a spot on the ground with my foot, jab the shovel in and scoop to make a hole, stick the tree in, get the roots hanging down straight, and step to pack the dirt in.

Now do it again. Again. And again.

The work was mind-numbing, and maybe that's why I loved it. Without my shovel, I was nothing. The only thing that mattered was finding a good spot for the next tree. To make money, I had to move through mud, rain, sleet, and scorching sun. I found that, regardless of the conditions, there was a power in my continuous action.

At the end of each planting day, I'd eat a mountain of food and pass out in my tent. It wasn't all perfect. There were complications. They came in the form of mosquitoes and blackflies, but also beer, boys, blisters, and bears.

A cinnamon bear started to hang out around our camp. She was named for the lighter colour of her coat. We were in an area of Ontario with a high concentration of black bears. Some of them may have been relocated from elsewhere. If they became dependent on people's food, eating from garbage dumps or robbing campers, they were caught in large steel culvert traps. They would be tranquilized, tagged, driven north, and then let go. I'd heard stories that some of the bears relocated in this way had returned to where they came from. The call of home was strong enough to lure them over hundreds of miles.

Others—like, I imagined, this cinnamon bear—tried to make a life where they were released. Even if this one hadn't been relocated, she was displaced after finding herself in a logged clear-cut. She didn't have many choices. She was stuck with us, a camp of about sixty people planting trees.

We kept our backpacks in the transport vans because the cinnamon bear loved peanut butter sandwiches even more than I did. One day someone left a window in the van rolled down about an inch too far. The cinnamon bear managed to thread her arm through the window, pop the lock, and get the door open. She raided our backpacks.

When I discovered my backpack had been taken, it felt like being mugged. We were in the middle of the bush; there was nowhere to buy another one until my day off, a week away. My backpack felt necessary to my survival. I used it to carry tape for my hands, bug juice, water, and food. I needed it.

I went trawling through the ditches along the road. Any depression or rock that looked like a place to hide, I went under, around, and through it.

After an hour I found my pack tucked into the stump of an old tree. When I saw the zipper was still closed, I felt a surge of hope. I thought maybe the bear had discarded the pack without robbing me, but then I took a second look. She hadn't bothered with the zipper. She made a new opening by sticking a claw in the fabric and pulling along exactly beside the zipper. The new slit followed over the top of the pack and made a perfect slash.

I opened the pack. It was empty. The Tupperware I used for my sandwiches wasn't there, so I looked around and found it behind the stump. The lid had been discarded a few feet away. An important piece of equipment, I was so glad to find it. Calorie consumption was vital. I ate at least six peanut butter sandwiches every day, and often closer to nine. The Tupperware kept them fluffy and dry, one small luxury in what were otherwise fairly brutal conditions.

I checked the Tupperware and turned the plastic over. It was intact and still in good condition, but empty. The sandwiches were gone, of course, but the bear hadn't destroyed the container. I couldn't understand how she had opened it, until I found one tiny mark. There was a single puncture in the red lid. She had stuck the end of her claw into the plastic to get purchase and pulled to lift the pliable plastic up.

At the time, I was mostly concerned about being nine sandwiches short for the day. If I hadn't been so hungry, I would have been impressed. This bear was clever.

With luck like that, the cinnamon bear started coming around our camp all the time. We'd blast music to scare her off, but she didn't mind that much. She found the grind of Metallica and the thump of Rage Against the Machine tolerable as long as there was also a cook shack with enough food for a week inside.

One night, I woke. Did I hear something? I sensed something in the air, like the static that comes with the presence of a big body. I heard sniffing from a larger nose. A shuffle and then a crunch. I sat straight up.

"Claire?" It was my friend Jackie, calling out from the tent beside me.

"Yeah?" I whispered.

The sound travelled as though there was nothing between us. My tent was made of a stretched piece of nylon strung between aluminum poles. Over that was a fly, also nylon, that was supposed to keep the water out but more often chose to dump it on me. It all felt way too flimsy, those two pieces of fabric between a sniffing nose and me.

There was a ripping sound and another crunch.

"Claire?" Jackie sounded scared this time, and that scared me because she's one of the bravest people I know. "Are you eating an apple?" she asked.

I almost laughed, but then I listened and understood her question. There was the distinct sound of teeth biting into crispy flesh. A sucking, like the juice might be slipping down a chin.

My imagination can be worse than the real thing, so I forced myself out of my sleeping bag to look. The temperatures kissed the freezing point that night and it was a struggle to get up. I unzipped my tent slowly and stuck my head out to look toward the crunching.

It took a minute for my eyes to adjust. Human eyesight isn't as good in the dark as that of many other mammals. Bears, like wolves and dogs, have a reflective layer in their eyes called the tapetum lucidum. This allows light to filter twice. It's the same layer that makes the eyes of animals shine at night. They can see more than we can. I felt my disadvantage acutely. I saw a shape moving by the Weatherhaven, the large tent where we ate. It was about fifty feet away. Not the cinnamon bear, but a bear.

The bear was about the size of a large dog, but heavier given the denser muscle. I don't know his sex, but I'll say he. He was tidy-looking, with a coat that glinted when it caught the light of the crescent moon. His movements were supple and slightly disorganized, like a kid's.

My fear dropped away. The bear reminded me more of a raccoon routing around near a garbage can than anything. If I stood up, I felt sure I could go toe to toe. But there was no need for that. The bear didn't care about me at all. He was busy with much better things.

Someone had left a box of apples on the table. This was a mistake. We lived by the rule that a fed bear often ends up as a dead bear. Humans don't tolerate much misbehaviour from wild animals. When a bear steps over a line by invading a house, garbage bin, or cottage, and learns that the reward is worth the risk, the story tends to end in one way: the bear ends up being trapped and relocated, or shot. It's far better not to give the opportunity for conflict to start.

I wasn't scared. Instead, I felt a sense of wonder.

I watched the bear for a while. Too long. I should have scared him off immediately. By letting him hang around, I risked sending him a message that humans weren't something to worry about.

What transfixed me were his movements—they were recognizably human. He took an apple out of the top of the box, looked at it, turned it in his dexterous hand, took a bite, then threw it over his shoulder. Then he dipped his hand into the box for the next apple. He kept doing this, inspecting, taking a bite, tossing, on to the next, as if he was only taking the best bite of each one. He did it with such clear intention, I could feel his excitement. What luck for a small bear to have a clear run at this cache of fruit when normally he would be chased away. I'm sure it was one of the best nights of that bear's life.

Mine too.

I woke up a few other people. Many of us slept with metal pots and lids at our feet for this reason. A few of us banged them and shouted. The small bear ran off.

The encounter wouldn't have occurred if we had properly secured our food, but otherwise, this is typical of the close encounters I've had with bears. Nothing happens.

Or maybe that's not quite correct. One significant thing did happen. I woke up the next morning with a full-blown bear obsession.

Alongside my fascination, a contradiction started turning over in my mind.

On the one hand, my experience of bears was that they were harmless and only wanted food, like this apple-eating bear. On the other, I had heard the tragic story around a campfire about the attack on Bates Island.

These two experiences pulled apart from each other. I couldn't reconcile them.

8.

RAY AND CAROLA ARRIVED at the island around 5:45 p.m. To the west, as they travelled, the sun lowered and the light flattened. They weren't too late, but it was cold and they wouldn't dawdle either. I'm sure they tried to arrive on the island well before dark. It had been a long day of travel. They had to make camp.

The sun set at 6:43 that evening.

I can't know exactly what happened next, but I can infer based on the evidence found at the campsite, and from camping in the park at that time of year.

The bow of the runabout nosed up to the thin strip of sand. It ground against the pebbles, a high-pitched squeal that only stopped when a hand steadied the boat. Water lapped against the metal side. She moved to the edge of the bow with a line of rope to pull the boat in her hand. One, two, three, she took a wild leap to the shore. She jumped wide to keep her feet dry.

A wet foot would only be temporary misery. Staying dry isn't a matter of survival in those temperatures, especially given that they had sleeping bags for warmth and the means to make a fire, but staying dry would be way more comfortable. She held the boat, pulling it closer while he moved to the front. With his weight grounding the bow, he stepped out. They took a quick look around and agreed, this was the campsite where they would spend the night.

There are three things that are essential when camping in most climates: water, shelter, and food. The first is the most important. "Thousands have lived without love, not one without water," wrote W.H. Auden.

As experienced campers, they both knew a person can survive for only about three days without water. But they were in the land of plenty. They could go to the lake to fill the pot. There were fewer boats or people around to pollute in 1991. The outlet of a river can deliver a parasite like giardia, but probably not at the island. The lake was deep and clear. From the boat, she could have dipped a mug into the lake and drunk it straight.

With water in good supply, this left food and shelter. She took the essentials from the boat—the stove, the hamburger meat in a Styrofoam tray, a lighter, and the pans. She set these down by the ring of rocks that marked the campfire. As he started to look for the tent in the boat, she would set the water boiling and then make dinner.

She returned to the campfire with a pot of water and turned the knob on the stove. The lighter, found later, was a Bic. To operate it, the thumb has to turn the round dial first and then hit the small red pad to produce a flame. It was tricky to get the thing lit, especially with fingers that were cold and stiff. On the third strike, the flame jumped. She touched it to the metal circle.

The stove was a Coleman. The invisible gas turned a brilliant blue as it caught around the ring. With the stove fired, the compressed gas came out as loud static, a hiss. It covered up any noises around her, but she didn't mind. The burning sent a ruddy heat to her cheek. The warmth was welcome.

She might have glanced up to see how he was doing. They had camped together many times. Setting up the site was like a choreographed performance. He unloaded some of their equipment from the boat. He had found the large sack stuffed with the tent.

When she lit the stove, she could no longer hear his footsteps over the hiss, but there was no need. She knew exactly what he was doing. He looked around the campsite to find the best flat spot for the tent.

While they would use the stove for cooking, she wanted to collect wood to have a fire later. The campers who came through in the busier summer season had already picked up the deadfall from the trees. She walked toward the back of the campsite, going deeper toward the centre ridge of the island, where the bush had been allowed to grow up and the trees were closer together. She found a downed branch and snapped it with her foot. A few smaller branches lay around and she scooped those into her arms. She saw a piece of birchbark on the ground. It was useful as a fire starter; when peeled back, the pink inner layers are thin enough to catch when touched by a flame. It would light like paper.

Meanwhile, near the shoreline, he pulled the nose of the boat up farther. Now nearly empty, only a few bags of groceries inside, it rode higher in the water. He didn't want it to float away. He made sure it was secure and, maybe, tied the bowline to a tree. He pushed his glasses up the bridge of his nose with a finger.

Tree roots held the bank like interlaced fingers and he climbed them, balancing to step to the spot he had in mind for the tent. Around the campfire, the pine needles were like a carpet. He inspected a second place farther back and one nearer the water. Each spot looked like a circle of flattened dirt and needles where other people had pitched their tents earlier in the season. He took his time to do his evaluation, wanting the one that was most level. Sleeping on an accidental slant can mean waking up with an unpleasant rush of blood to the head. If it rained, they wanted good drainage to make sure water would run away from the base of the tent.

He returned to the first spot he found by the large pine at the front of the campsite, stood there, and looked out. Soon the sun would start to set.

He sensed something, maybe movement, but it was more like a feeling. A shape or a smell, but he wasn't sure what. He glanced toward the back of the campsite and looked at the dark spaces between the trees.

With an armful of wood, she had turned back toward the fire. For a moment, she stopped. She had a strange sensation, a kind of heat on her skin. It was like she was being watched, but she knew there was no other party on the island. She couldn't quite place the feeling. She turned to look into the trees.

There was a campsite beside them. It wasn't close, but it also hugged the shoreline, and from where she stood, she might be able to see if another group had pulled up. Away from the stove, she might hear their voices or the clang of a paddle against a canoe.

Water carries sounds across it, voices skip, and laughter rings out. She squinted through the trees and saw nothing. It was silent.

There were no other people for miles around.

The light came into the campsite at a hard angle. At that time of year, the darkening seemed to accelerate toward the end of the day. She ran her eyes along the trees and through the dark spaces between them. She had a sense that something was there, but quickly corrected herself. This was silly—the mind playing tricks. The pressing feeling was of the dark coming. It was only telling her to hurry up and make dinner. She walked back to the campfire ring.

He had a similar feeling. It was easy to feel on edge the first night of camping in the wilderness. His body hadn't quite relaxed into the slower rhythm of the lake and camping life. The mind was still in the city, anxious and darting. He almost laughed when he looked more carefully toward the back of the campsite and saw her returning. She had wood in her arms for the campfire later. He admired her as she crouched to place the bundle she had collected beside the fire.

She checked the stove. The water had boiled. She put the pot to the side and replaced it with the pan on the one ring of the Coleman stove. They had brought fresh food for this night only. With no electricity, it wouldn't stay good for longer. But that night, they would have a feast: the small fish they'd caught on the way, or brought, as an appetizer, then burgers, tomatoes, and cheese. For the next few days, though, they had bought things that would keep.

She put the Styrofoam tray of ground beef on a rock beside the campfire.

Dinner would be ready soon. He caught the scent of fish. He salivated. It had been a long day. He took the tent out and slid the poles through the fabric. He was good at this, quick, having done it many times. Soon the nylon stretched tight around the frame. He adjusted it to move the door to face the water. When they woke up, they would unzip the tent and have a view of the lake.

He would leave the sleeping bags wrapped up until later. It wasn't raining, but at that time of year the weather could turn on a dime, and he didn't want to risk them getting wet. He took out one of the air mattresses, turned the plug, and blew into it. Only a lungful of air was needed and the cushion expanded an inch or so in thickness, but the effort still left him light-headed. He steadied himself, head swimming slightly, then turned to put the mattress inside. This meant stretching farther from the door. He was almost lying down because he didn't want to bring the dirt from his shoes inside the tent. He looked over to find the second mattress and reached for it.

That's when he heard it, a deep vibration.

Something had changed outside the tent, and he couldn't imagine what. She called out, a sound that was a cross between a scream and a moan. It was a noise unlike any he'd ever heard her make before. His mind scrambled to catch up, but for a moment he couldn't make sense of the tear in their reality.

There was something on the island with them. They weren't alone.

9.

IT WAS JUNE, THE spring before the attack. The bear had fattened, but he was still hungry. His active hours were filled with the restless and relentless search for food. Always hungry. A scent slipped past his nose, carrying moisture, dense with some heavier particles, and these made him curious.

A few more sniffs and soon he knew what it was. A moose was farther upstream, a female, and she was feeding. He caught the snap of branches breaking between her lips. And there was something else. He lifted his snout and took a long draw in.

He started moving toward it to investigate.

A full-grown moose can appear awkward or lazy. They often look passive and amble along as though they are in no rush. Sometimes they rest on cloven hooves when standing or wallow in a mucky pond. Like a cow, they chew cud, regurgitated food that they bring back up for a second round of digestion. These docile-looking moments might be a reason that some people underestimate them.

Moose can be vicious. When something encroaches on their personal space, they can charge. They are fierce defenders of their young. Their hooves are sharp. Jeremy Inglis, the wildlife biologist, described the capabilities of these weapons. He had secured a radio collar around a bear's neck, which he later found on the ground. It was made from a thick leather strap. A moose had been in an altercation with the bear and, using her sharp front hoof, cut the leather strap straight through.

By this time in the spring, the bear had wandered farther away from his den. He moved west and north in the general direction of his usual food sources. The scent of a calf wasn't unexpected. Bear and moose often spend time in the same fertile patches of forest close to mature stands of trees. The food in this type of habitat attracted them all. Run-ins were likely.

The bear was an opportunistic hunter. If a chance for meat came within sniffing distance, he would take time to investigate. He weighed his chances carefully. Would the reward of hunting be worth the risk he'd have to take? Most of the time, it wasn't. His judgment changed with the season, the level of frost that spring, the condition of the animals around him, and his own stores of fat and muscle. To survive as a wild bear means engaging in a constant calculus.

The moose calf had been born more than a month before. She was lucky to make it through the first days of her life, especially given the pack of wolves who roamed in that part of the park. The wolves knew of her birth, but after a run-in with this same mother moose a few years before, they made a strategic decision to keep their distance.

The calf weighed only about twenty-eight pounds at birth. For the first few days she was weak and extremely vulnerable. Her large eyes were blinking and cloudy. Her long legs were folded and clumsy. Her mother kept a careful watch while she tried to arrange her limbs in a way that would take her weight. She could swim within a few hours of birth, but it took a few days before she could run.

The calf made it through those first precarious days because her mother stayed vigilant. The calf grew on milk. She would be fully grown in a few years (many calves don't live that long). Dave Taylor, in his book about black bears, cites studies in Idaho, Alaska, Saskatchewan, and Quebec that show bears are responsible for about one-third of calf mortality.

This calf had put on a pound or two a day and was now roughly the size of an adult human.

The bear was more than a mile away, but he didn't rely on his eyes. When he first caught the visual signs of two bodies, marked by twitching branches, the pattern matched the scents he knew. They stood in the muck near a flooded area, the vegetation made lush by the water of a beaver pond, and were stripping leaves from a tree.

The bear crouched, covered by the thick brush. When looking at potential prey, a bear will stay low, near silent, and downwind. "It's quiet," bear expert Stephen Herrero told the *New York Times* when asked about the approach of a black bear with predatory motivations. "It stalks you just like a lion might stalk you."

I CAN'T ASK THE moose or the calf what this moment was like, but Tom Walter experienced something similar. From Waterford, Michigan, Tom flew in to go fishing with his brother east of Lake Superior, Ontario. They were in a boat when Tom asked to be dropped off on shore. He had his video camera and wanted to capture footage of a moose they had spotted. His brother agreed to return in an hour.

Just after the boat motored off, Tom heard a sound close by.

Instinctively, Tom pointed his camera in the direction of the sound. As a black bear approached, he filmed it. Think of how a cat moves quietly over the ground; they have soft pads on their paws, they put a foot down in silence. Any sounds were made by the brush of leaves, a bending branch, or the snap of a twig under the bear's foot.

It was spring. The camera's lens caught some of the surroundings, leaves on the ground, browned and soggy after a long winter. New growth hadn't started budding. It looked cold and bare all around them. Food wasn't abundant yet. This bear was probably hungry.

Tom's first thought was, "Wow, this is cool. I'm going to get a black bear on my videotape." He expected the bear to run away.

But the bear didn't run. He moved slowly toward Tom. The next shot shows the bear with his head low, glancing up to keep track of his prey. The bear kept following Tom, slowly working to close the distance between them.

"Go on, bear!" Tom shouted. His voice cracked, raw and uneven. The camera flashed by his face to show wide eyes. Tom had no doubt that this was trouble. He kept shouting, "Go away, bear!"

When the camera panned back to the bear, he kept his head low, ducking back into the frame, almost looking playful, always testing. But it is menacing.

Tom walked through the woods backwards, trying to put distance between them but not wanting to take his eyes off the bear.

The land he moved through was undulating and rough. There was no trail. He tripped on sticks and rocks, trying to stay upright, moving awkwardly, scared. Crucially, he didn't turn and run.

"Git," Tom yelled.

The ground swirled by the lens. The leaves, the sky, a flash of a bush, the camera whipped around, and there was the bear again. This time much larger in the frame. Closer. The bear pressed forward and closed the gap. Tom said he held the camera out because it was something he could keep between them. This means that when the bear looked up, he glanced directly into the lens. The picture freezes.

The bear stares at Tom from below, ears perked forward, a look of intent.

In the footage, looking into the bear's eyes, I see intelligence. There is interest, curiosity, and intention. These are the eyes of a skilled opportunist, an animal weighing his chances.

For the bear stalking Tom, killing would necessarily be intimate. The bear would have to get up close. His teeth were a weapon. His claws would be involved. Few human hunters would take the risk of walking closer and closer to any large mammal.

The bear continued to push Tom backwards, ducking and weaving, trying to find the man's limits. One thing that strikes me about watching this footage is the lack of aggression the bear showed. There was no growling, huffing, pawing, or any of the things a black bear does when feeling defensive. What the bear showed was determined persistence. His movements were measured and easy. He was pressing consistently, but not in a hurry. He looked willing to follow Tom for as long as it took.

Tom was certain the bear wasn't going to stop pursuing him unless something changed in the equation. When he saw his brother in the boat, he found a way out. He shouted and waved, the boat came over, and Tom jumped in. With the aid of an engine, they put distance between themselves and the bear. Tom was safe.

THE BEAR MIGHT HAVE crept up on the mother moose and her calf using a similar kind of approach. Maybe the calf heard a snap, from a broken twig when the bear set his soft paw on the ground and eased the full weight of his body onto it.

If the mother moose was worried, she didn't show it at first. She allowed the bear to close the distance a little more, but the moose wasn't complacent either. She nosed her calf up onto the firmer ground. The boldness of this bear was unusual. He was large, with rounded muscles and a glossy coat. The moose knew what this meant about his health and ability.

The mother moose had size on her side. She took a different tactic and charged at the bear. She did this without too much effort. Her heartbeat stayed relatively stable. She was just over seven hundred pounds. From ground to shoulder, she stood just over five and a half feet. She was more than twice the size of the bear.

When the mother moose charged, the bear backed off. He kept his distance, but continued to watch the calf. He wanted to get between them. If he could separate the two, then he could close in around the vulnerable baby.

The mother returned to stripping leaves from a branch with her dexterous lips. She could eat at least sixty pounds of this kind of food in a day.

After a time, the bear approached again. Slowly. He was more stubborn than any of the black bears this moose had encountered. He started to close the space between them again. She ignored him at first, so he closed it a little more.

The calf became alarmed and tucked in behind her mother's haunches. The long ears on the calf were alert, quivering, twitching. She was skittish, but she felt safer once touching her mother's warm stomach with a soft muzzle. She knew it was important to stay close. Her life depended on it.

This encouraged the bear. He saw the fattened haunches on the calf and grew a little bolder. His nervous system responded to the new stimulation—the increased heartbeat, muscle contractions, the running blood, all these came to him like encouraging vibrations. The scents stimulated the saliva in his mouth, the memory of meat.

Years before, Jerry had witnessed the aftermath of a fight between a bear and a moose at Opeongo Lake. The moose had jumped into the water to get away from a bear. When Jerry went to see what was going on, he found an injured calf with a broken leg and hip and all sorts of scratches. The bear had jumped on the back of the calf and tried to bite the neck. The bear had cracked the calf's spine but had not managed to sever the spinal cord. The calf ended up dying from the injuries.

Not wanting a similar outcome, the mother moose turned toward the bear again. The black hairs that ran along her spine prickled and stood up. Her long ears lay back. She licked her lips and narrowed her eyes. This time she charged and delivered a more serious warning to the bear. She could stomp or kick with enough power to snap his neck.

The bear saw the health and strength of this moose and took his cue. The protein the calf would provide as food wasn't worth bloodshed. If he tried to hunt the moose calf, he would undoubtedly be injured, and possibly end up dead.

The bear scampered away.

His attempts to hunt often ended in failure, but he had lived for eight seasons by then. He was still alive because he knew where to go for his next meal. He consoled himself by eating some grubs that evening.

In the morning, he woke up even hungrier. The memory of being unable to secure a feast of meat came as a hollow sensation in the belly. The near miss made him more determined. He stood, the pads of his paws spreading to take his weight, stretched, shook, and started his search.

A craving settled like a heavy stone in his belly. Only meat would relieve it.

Part Four

KEEP YOUR DISTANCE

10.

I SAT ON A ledge of a glacier. A man named Dave chipped out a spot with his ice axe and wiggled in to sit beside me. I gave him one of my chocolate chip cookies.

Dave talks in the measured speech of someone born and bred in California. He is handsome with sandy blond hair, the freckles of his Irish heritage. Tall and lean, a natural athlete, though it was clear that his concerns were more about function than form. His jacket was patched with silver duct tape repairs. He had sewn a rip in his ski pants with dental floss. We talked about E. Bradford Burns's theory of progress in Latin America, how lenticular clouds are shaped by winds when warm and cool air meet, and the use of all caps in *A Prayer for Owen Meany* by John Irving, three things I'd never had the chance to discuss in one conversation, and especially not while wearing crampons.

At that time, we both lived itinerant lives, alternating between guiding courses and climbing excursions. Within a few weeks I lugged my hockey bag of gear into the back of Dave's car, a 1978 Datsun wagon. He called her Bluey, and the two of them were tight. I understood the size of the gesture when Dave cleared the passenger seat for me. He threw away a capped Pepsi bottle that held pee ("a traveller"), then tossed a tin of chewing tobacco and his climbing rope into the back seat.

Bluey didn't have air conditioning. Instead, to cool herself, she blew hot air from her engine on my legs. She didn't like going over fifty miles an hour. The three of us drove through the desert, slowly, to Joshua Tree to go rock climbing.

For a person who had grown up in a land of lakes, the desert was a different planet. I was often thirsty. My lips stayed puckered until my body adapted. I loved how the sun didn't let anything hide, the scent of juniper and sage hanging in the stark relief. Everything was solid and dry. The tough stalk of a plant looked as if it had earned its place.

At night the dark let the cold rush in.

We went climbing on rough granite rocks. As we became more accustomed to the conditions, we started doing harder routes. One day, Dave led a difficult pitch. I was on belay, holding the end of the rope that was tied into my harness, with my brake hand tight around my hip. I craned my neck to watch as he climbed the tricky crux. His toe balanced on a small chip of stone. His chalked fingers held on by two tips. The face of the rock sat hard against his chest and he was about to move over a slight protrusion, an overhang. He reached his right arm above his head. I watched the muscle of his shoulders flex. And then his fingertips slipped.

It happened slowly at first.

Both Dave's hands came off the rock. Gravity took hold. His upper body bent back. I immediately understood that he was falling and there was no way to recover. He had placed a piece of protective gear in a crack in the rock above him. It should have caught the rope; instead, it popped out. His body flipped around.

Now he was falling headfirst toward a flat shelf of rock below him. That was when everything sped up.

My right hand was on the end of the rope. Dave had at least sixty pounds on me and is six inches taller. I didn't really understand the weight of his muscle until then, maybe because he is gentle. As the belayer, it was my job to brake and stop the rope running through our systems. This was the only way to prevent him from falling farther. If he did, he would hit the rock shelf, about thirty feet below. That distance was quickly closing.

A climbing rope is dynamic and stretches when it takes body weight. Because the protective piece popped out, there was too much slack in our system. I knew there was a chance he might hit the shelf. There was only one thing to do.

When his weight hit the rope, I held on tight.

I was ripped off my feet. I should have been tied in, my harness attached to something on the ground to hold me down. I wasn't because we thought of ourselves as equals. We should have been wearing helmets, but weren't because it was the nineties and we were stupid. Or maybe it was because we were young and falling in love—as close to invincible as a person can be.

Dave's weight caught the rope. I went shooting into the air.

The next thing I knew, the rock wall was directly in front of my face. There was a splotch of blood on the granite where my cheek had smashed. I barely felt it. I looked down and saw the climbing shoes on my feet, the sticky rubber and pointed toes, dangling off the ground. My right hand was still on the rope, braking, holding. I hadn't let go.

I swung from the momentum and blinked once. So focused on my hand holding the rope, it was hard to take in anything else. Then the reality of our situation started to settle. If I was hanging in the air, swaying, moving in an arc, physics must be working in our favour. Dave must be hanging too.

I looked up to see him dangling on the rope above me. The harness had caught and flipped him right side up a few feet before he hit the shelf. His face was distorted, a line of chalk across it, and he was gasping for breath. There was blood smeared on his teeth. A bloody lip, that was it.

That evening, we sat together and watched the desert turn pink. We drank warm Schlitz from cans. I called it moose piss, and he laughed. When the cold air came in, I moved to sit between his legs and leaned against his chest. The skin of his hands was rough from climbing. His fingertips rested on the bare skin of my neck. Through the calluses from the rock, I could feel warmth. He was bigger, I accepted it. The bloody graze on my cheek confirmed it. His forearms had layers of muscle with one vein that ran down. His pulse was slower and he is always calmer. He lives in the moment. My exhale fell into line with his and I noticed that his breathing could steady mine.

SOON AFTER, WE WERE married. We moved to San Francisco, then London, England, and back to Toronto, where we started collecting things: a sofa, shoes that needed polishing, two cats, many books, and three sad-looking plants.

Time passed. We had two sons.

When the boys were three and six years old, we took them into the backcountry of Algonquin Park. Briefly, I worried it was a dangerous or reckless place for a holiday, but then reminded myself about the slim chances of a bear attack. I bought bear spray, a kind of aerosol pepper spray like mace. It can be a helpful tool if a bear comes too close.

I taught Dave how to use the bear spray. I had him practise the actions of taking the safety band off and pointing the can. It's all too easy to point the nozzle in the wrong direction, or toward the wind, and spray yourself by mistake.

Bear spray expires. It's important to check the date. The biologist Mike Wilton had a can that he worried was beyond its useful life. He decided to check the strength of the spray by aiming the nozzle into a toilet. When we spoke, he warned me, while laughing, against ever trying this method for testing. The spray hit the bowl with such force, it came back and caught him in the face. It took hours to recover.

Dave and I agreed that we'd travel with the canister on a belt and then keep it in a prominent place in camp, but I wasn't worried on the drive up to Algonquin Park. I had phoned the warden's office and asked if there had been any trouble with the bears that year. I always ask people who have worked and lived in the area for an update before I go camping, even in a place I know. I've never come across anyone who lives in proximity to bears who doesn't enjoy talking about them.

The park office had assured me that the bears had plenty to eat. It was a good year for berries. Provided we kept a clean camp, there was no obvious reason to worry about my kids even if they were round and plump, perfect little snacks.

We put the boys in life jackets and stacked them in the middle of the canoe, the most delicate luggage. Dave and I had been travelling together in the backcountry for more than ten years, but this time our load was much heavier than on previous trips. The range of things we deemed necessary had expanded exponentially, including marshmallows, tiny socks, toy cars, and a teddy bear who answered to the name Celeste.

We parked in the gravel lot at the Algonquin Outfitters store on Opeongo Lake. The large lake and services made for easier backcountry access with kids. At the time, I didn't think of the couple. Their story didn't touch me during the day back then. It still lived, mostly, in the realm of my imagination. I'd only think about it when I was alone, or in the dark.

We paddled out onto Opeongo Lake and found a campsite with graceful rocks at the front. I laid my hand on the smooth granite, which still held heat from the day. The sun started to lower, softening everything around us. The trees rolled along beside the lake and dipped into valleys as if each root linked one life to the next.

I checked the campsite for anything that might attract bears—a berry bush, a pile of garbage, a rodent carcass. I looked for signs that a bear might have been on the campsite—digging, broken branches, scratches on a tree, hair or scat. Bear scat looks like a pile of human feces, which isn't as strange as it sounds; we have similar-sized digestive tracks. The scat will change depending on what the bear has been eating, but there are sometimes obvious clues. Whereas a human diet tends to be processed, a bear might excrete bits of berries or plants, hair from carrion, or leaves and twigs.

I'm always on the lookout for bear tracks, but finding them is rare. Fresh mud, snow, sand, and loose dirt are good places to look. I study bear tracks in hopes I'll be ready to do an identification when I come across one. Bears' hips wiggle when they walk. This means the rear foot will be placed on top of or in front of the lead print. If a bear is running, the prints will be much farther apart. But there were no signs of bears on our campsite.

All I spotted was a chipmunk.

I showed our older son, Ben, how to whittle a stick with a pocket knife. He has the darker hair of my mother, he's a busy person, his nose is pointed in the direction of his curiosity. The glint of the sharp metal held his attention for hours. He was careful and knew the weight of the blade was a measure of responsibility. He made a perfect point, an arrow. We sealed the tip in the hot coals of the fire. Then we started making a bow. I thought it would be good for fighting dragons if they came to the campsite. He said it was more likely to be zombies.

Our younger son, Max, has my blond hair and has longer limbs and can be found sitting still much more often than his brother. He prefers to keep things steady and survived the whole trip on bread with butter. He didn't trust vegetables in general and he preferred for things to remain as predictable as possible. As a concession to his sense of order, we brought his toy cars along. He spent much of his time sitting beside a flat rock. He sorted the cars into a line. Once they were perfectly positioned, he would brush the dirt from his small hands and say, "Done." Then he would quickly get to work on making a new traffic jam facing in the opposite direction.

Ben picked a leech off his ankle. He wasn't grossed out because he didn't know he should be. He held it out between his fingers to show me. "Is the leech bleeding?"

I explained it had been drinking his blood.

He squinted up close at the engorged black body. "That's a strange breakfast," he said.

We fished and caught nothing. The bass perfected their ability to outsmart us. They had seen the likes of our de-barbed hooks and worms many times before.

I burned the rice, as I often do.

A few nights into the trip, I sat by the water with Max after dinner. I asked how he'd felt when we paddled the day before. We had been in the middle of the lake and, seeing the threat of lightning, pulled over to a small island. It had rained hard. We watched a lightning storm rip across the water, while huddling under a tarp to wait out the storm. "I felt scared in my body," Max told me. "But I'm safe because Dad and you are here."

At twilight, I started to think about securing the camp. I knew that keeping our distance from bears was best done by securing our food. Along with the canoe, we had rented a large plastic container called a bear barrel. We put all the food and garbage inside, including anything with an intriguing scent, like a cup with juice at the bottom, toothpaste, sunscreen, and soap.

Years before, my friends had a tent ripped apart by a bear. They couldn't understand why the bear had shredded it so thoroughly, until, while picking through the rubble, they uncovered a tube of toothpaste that had been split down the middle with a claw and licked clean. Anything with a scent can be an attraction. Bears aren't picky.

A friend had a bear break into his cottage. The fridge had been opened, but it had already been emptied and cleaned. There was nothing to eat inside it. The bear had entered a back cupboard, found blue paint, and eaten that. All he left behind was a trail of blue poop.

In a popular camping spot like Algonquin Park, or one as busy as Yosemite or Yellowstone, a barrel isn't always sufficient. If bears are clever enough to forage food through the seasons, they can apply that same intelligence to learning, adapting, and changing tactics to open our containers. This was a lesson I had learned while being robbed of my peanut butter sandwiches while tree planting.

Another friend was deep in the backcountry of Quebec. They went to bed having hung a food barrel in their camp and woke to find a bear pulling it down from the tree. The last they saw of the barrel, it was in the mouth of the bear, who ran off with it. They never found it.

Sometimes a campsite will have a board nailed across two trees, or an improvised structure called a bear hang. The idea is to pack your food and suspend it so a bear can't get to it, but they are adept at climbing trees. They can hang on to a branch with one arm and reach farther than I ever thought. A smaller tree that will support the weight of the food, but not the bear, is best. It should be a good distance from the campsite, at least a hundred feet.

Our campsite didn't have a hang, but I had a rope. I tied a rock in a small stuff sack to one end. I threw this over the branch of a tree, then hoisted our food barrel up about twelve feet in the air, with more rope dangling from it. Once it was hanging in the air, I used this second rope to pull it away from the first tree trunk. It should be clear of the trunk by at least six feet.

Once we had hung the food, Dave lowered his voice so the boys wouldn't hear. "Will that keep the bears away?"

I knew why he was asking. I'd told him the story of what happened on Opeongo Lake. "I don't think the couple stored their food properly," I said. "That's why the bear approached the island." At the time, I believed this was true.

I KEEP NOTEBOOKS. I had looked at a few before the trip. They have the influence of Algonquin Park all over them. One page describes how the tips of the trees become increasingly pointy as you drive north from Toronto. Another paragraph talks about how the legs on a moose are unfeasibly long and their elbows point to the sky. I turned the page and found a quote from Jessica Zafra about how the body is just the meat you live in, and a photo of Barack Obama laughing. I wrote about how he seems to have the right attitude for life, with a cut-out of a quote by Dave Barry that appeared in *Slate*: "A sense of humour is a measurement of the extent to which we realize that we are trapped in a world almost totally devoid of reason."

In my notebooks, there are many photos of bears. Some passages describe how I'm acutely aware that my feelings about bears radiate in an outward direction only. For all the time I've spent thinking about bears, I'm convinced they spend little time on me. When their attention has been turned in my direction, there is a lack of drama. For all the times I've encountered a bear and written down their reaction, it's only wary, indifferent, or avoidant. Where I have attracted more attention, it's not about me. It's my food.

One other thing is consistent: I note bears are mysterious. The most unknowable things are the ones that hold the attention over a lifetime—a mountain, ghosts, stars, or bears. Mystery drives an endless curiosity.

That night in Algonquin Park, the sunset stretched across the sky, the colours so deep and sharp it looked as though the horizon was bleeding.

When the dark settled in, Dave and I each sat with a warm boy on our lap. I lit a fire using only one match, to show off. We stared into the flames. I told a version of *Beowulf* as the bedtime story. With round eyes we stared into the fire, listening, breathing quietly, crackling flames reaching up, the night lying outside the circle of light. *Beowulf* comes from a time when stories were told as part of an oral tradition. Each time it's told, a story is slightly altered to fit the situation the storyteller finds herself in. Not wanting to spook the boys before bed, I focused the story on Grendel and played up his lonely outcast traits. I twisted the tale into a story about how Grendel wanted friends.

The boys were heavy and relaxed by the end of my story. We tucked them into the sleeping bags and zipped the tent shut.

I stripped down and dipped into the black water of the lake. Dave silently slipped in beside me. After a night swim, we sat by the fire, naked and wrapped together in a sleeping bag to warm up. I grabbed his flannel shirt and pulled it on.

We crawled quietly into the tent, not wanting to wake the boys. I turned on my headlamp to sneak a peek at them. Both had slack cheeks, mouths open, and dirt smudged on their noses. Ben had a crust of marshmallow in the corner of his mouth. They slept with the peacefulness that comes after fresh air and a full day.

We curled on either side of the small bodies. Dave reached out to place his palm gently on my head, a quiet promise. Keeping the boys safe between us felt like the right way to be out there, perched on the edge of the land, near the water, our tent pitched on a blanket of pine needles. We assumed that we would sleep side by side for many years to come.

Dave always falls asleep the moment his head makes contact with a pillow. I lie awake, turning and twisting. I listened to the sounds outside the tent. I thought about bears. The night was quiet outside the thin layer of nylon. I listened for the smallest sounds, the water licking the rocks, the faint chirp of a faraway frog, and a mosquito humming in my ear. I was aware these sounds were not the ones I was listening for.

The bears had plenty to eat. They wouldn't risk bothering with two stringy parents or their softer children. Even our marshmallows were gone by that point. We had a clean camp.

But still, I lay awake listening, staring at the pattern the light of the moon made through the branches, shining through the fabric of our tent. I started thinking about a detail of the Bates Island attack I'd read in one of my notebooks before the trip—the Styrofoam tray of ground beef.

Like most campsites in Algonquin Park, ours had a ring of rocks around the fire. While making dinner that evening, I had placed food on one of the largest rocks, using it like a countertop.

In 1991, the search party arrived at the campsite five days after the attack. They found the ground beef, still untouched, on the rock. Before that night, I'd always considered this proof that the couple mishandled their food. I assumed the bear was probably lured to the island by the tray of ground beef.

Twenty years later, while lying in the tent, I realized that the idea of the bear going to the island because he was attracted by food didn't add up. If he wanted the couple's food, why did the search party find the ground beef sitting on a rock five days later?

11.

BLACK BEARS TEND TO attack in daylight. Between when Ray and Carola arrived at the island, 5:45 p.m. or later, and before dark, the couple became aware that a bear was on the island with them.

Stephen Herrero, the wildlife biologist, is one of the world's foremost experts on bear attacks. His work has changed the conversation about bears in general and black bears specifically. In his book *Bear Attacks: Their Causes and Avoidance*, he writes, "Your best weapon to minimize the risk of a bear attack is your brain."

Ray's best chance for survival lay in his response, which depended on the kind of bear in front of him. Different species of bear have evolved different strategies for survival. At a glance, Ray would see the bear's black coat, but black bears are often confused with their larger cousins, brown or grizzly bears. Colour isn't a reliable way to distinguish the two. Black bears can have lighter coats, brown at the flanks, sometimes almost blond or cinnamon. Some black bears are even white.

Grizzly coat colours are equally varied. These bears can look blacker after they shed, but they can also be blond, cinnamon, or white. "Grizzled" refers to the white-tipped hair some grizzlies have on their back and shoulders. From a distance, these hairs will change in colour depending on their surroundings.

Grizzly is a popular umbrella term, but they are a sub-species of brown bears. All brown bears are generally larger than black bears, but size isn't necessarily a reliable way to tell the species apart. Some adult female grizzlies can weigh between 200 and 350 pounds, putting them in a similar weight category to the black bear that was on Bates Island.

Grizzlies are larger and more aggressive, which makes them more dangerous. However, much of their behaviour can also be interpreted as defensive. In most defensive moves, the bear won't make contact. But when they do, they have claws four inches long. A swipe can be deadly. Grizzlies cause about twice the human fatalities that black bears do.

A better way to tell the difference between a black bear and a grizzly is body shape. A grizzly has a distinct hump between the front shoulders. Their facial profile is more concave, like a dish. They have proportionally smaller and rounder ears. A black bear has no hump between the shoulders, a straighter facial profile, and relatively larger ears.

Ray didn't need to squint to see the bear's colour, ear shape, or shoulders. There aren't any grizzly or brown bears in Ontario. Only black bears live in Algonquin Park.

The population of black bears is growing in many places. There are around one million black bears in the world, and about 750,000 of those live in North America, with half in the United States. Black bears live in varied climates throughout

Canada, though they don't go to the regions farthest north. They make occasional excursions around the edges of a large city or suburb. They live in the northeast and northwest of the US, in places like Montana, North Carolina, and Oregon. There are populations in Florida and Texas. In 2019, a trail camera in the Sierra Gorda recorded the first evidence of a black bear in central Mexico in a hundred years.

As the black bear population grows, keeping a distance gets more difficult. Given what happened that evening, is it reasonable to think the couple misjudged the danger when they left the dock?

Based on statistics, Carola did take a substantial risk by going on that trip, but the danger didn't come from bears. Every woman who lives with a man is at risk. Romantic partners or family members kill over half the women murdered in the United States. In Canada, the numbers are counted differently but end up much the same. Worldwide, it's estimated that a woman or girl is killed by someone in her family every eleven minutes.

To be clear, there were no reports, not even a suggestion, of trouble in the couple's relationship. Domestic violence probably wasn't a threat to Carola, but there was another high-risk activity that both of them engaged in that day: they drove to Algonquin Park in a car. Around 1.3 million people die yearly worldwide in traffic accidents. Between 20 and 50 million people suffer non-fatal injuries.

Once the couple arrived, there were more likely ways to die in a wilderness park. Figures from a 2004–2005 survey by the Centers for Disease Control and Prevention give a range of what could go wrong: cardiovascular disease was the top killer, with

856,030 deaths; transportation accidents came a distant second, at 48,441; and drowning was way back in third, at 3,582. From there the numbers plummeted. Hypothermia, or freezing to death, was at 699, bee stings at 49, and snake bites, 5.

At the very end of the CDC's list was death by bear attack. In the year their figures were recorded, there were two.

Algonquin Park puts effort into giving visitors a basic education about bears. There are photos of black bears in the park offices and on the website. Pamphlets are sprinkled throughout all the tourist spots. They tell you how to handle your food and what to do if you see a bear. Rick Stronks, the chief park naturalist of Algonquin Park, talks to hundreds of visitors every year. He said, "Very few people who have knowledge about black bears are terrified of them."

People who have seen black bears in the wild, at a campsite, or near the edges of a town tend to have had experiences like mine. If they see a bear, they make a noise and the bear runs off. Most bears want to keep their distance from us.

Ray had seen at least one black bear before. His friend Regan told me they had gone camping together when they were younger and stayed on Opeongo Lake. A bear came into their campsite and hung around. He started chewing on the lid of the privy box. The friends didn't panic, but they were heedful. The dark made them feel vulnerable. They huddled around the fire, which "got progressively bigger as the night went on."

Regan said that the black bear on their campsite was scary, but that there wasn't a reason for great alarm. "It pretty much ignored us." Their food was safely hung in a tree. They waited for a long time. At some point in the night, the bear slipped away.

The evening on Bates Island, Ray knew this was a black bear. He was on an island, which made it difficult to keep his distance. One thing to do in this situation is talk. You don't have to sound aggressive, but you want the bear to know what you are: human. When I see a black bear, I say hello. I introduce myself. If I can, I explain to the bear that I'll be the one to give him space. This kind of chit-chat keeps the fear from my voice.

If talking doesn't work, or you can't leave, make more noise. Grab a pot and lid and bang them together. Hit a stick against a rock. Let the black bear know you are not prey. Nor are you small. You are tall. Stand up with your arms out. If you have something to hand, a shovel, an axe that you use for chopping wood, hold it up. Look big. Not like a moose calf or a deer fawn, not at all. You may not have a sharp-hooved moose mother standing beside you, but that doesn't mean you are easy pickings.

At some point, whether almost immediately or after trying to deter the bear, Ray would have realized this bear was different. Maybe more aggressive or persistent than he had seen in the past. The bear may have been less wary. He may have come closer. Maybe he was bolder.

When I asked Herrero, the bear expert, if there was anything else the couple could have done at this point to prevent the attack, he didn't hesitate. "Pepper spray," he said. In a study, Herrero found that in four of four encounters with an aggressive, surprised, or possibly predacious black bear, the spray "appeared to stop the behaviour the bear was displaying immediately prior to being sprayed."

A NATURE PHOTOGRAPHER, CURTIS Matwishyn, encountered a black bear at a popular hiking spot near Prince Albert, Saskatchewan. It's a case study of the use of bear spray. The footage Curtis posted online shows the bear curious, interested, and moving closer. Curtis held the bear spray canister up with the safety latch removed and the nozzle pointed in the bear's direction. "I'm leaving," he told the bear.

In the video, the bear's approach did not appear to be aggressive. He didn't pop his jaws, woof, or growl. There was no show of teeth, and he looked almost playful, except when he climbed a little way up a tree. From the higher vantage, the bear fixed his eyes on Curtis. I see intent. The bear was calculating his chances.

As the bear crept closer, Curtis decided it was time. He let out a squirt of spray; it sounded like a short hiss. His aim was perfect: it hit the bear in the eyes.

The bear immediately turned and hopped in the opposite direction, only pausing to bat at his irritated eyes. Curtis let out a relieved whoop. He made it safely back to his car. The bear spray was negative reinforcement. It not only stopped the approach but might deter this bear from approaching humans in the future.

When Curtis was asked by a podcaster, James Alofs, if he would have done anything differently, Curtis said he wished he'd brought his air horn. The loud honk is often enough to send a bear running. He also wondered if he should have used the spray earlier. Maybe, but a regular canister only sprays for less than ten seconds. It's nice to have some left in the can.

Would Curtis have been better off with a gun?

It's illegal to carry a gun in a national park in Canada, but under the video there's a long debate about using guns for protection. A study looked at bear encounters involving 172 people. About 70 percent of the incidents involved grizzlies; the rest were black bears and two polar bears. The study compared using bear spray with firing a gun, and found that spray stopped aggressive bear behaviour in 92 percent of cases. Guns were effective 67 percent of the time.

The bear spray works, in part, because it gives a person a reason to stand their ground. Running away from a bear is the worst possible choice, as it can trigger a chase response.

Accuracy is a problem with a gun. The data suggests that it takes an average of four shots to stop a bear. There are many stories of people shooting other members of their party. When a grizzly attacked a hunter in Montana in 2011, a friend with a gun stepped in to help. The attacked man died, not of injuries from the bear, but from a single gunshot wound to the chest. Of course, friendly fire can happen with bear spray too, but while the results are unpleasant, they aren't deadly.

RAY DIDN'T HAVE BEAR spray. I don't remember many people carrying it in the 1990s.

At this point, if Ray was near or around the tent, the nylon walls would have been no match for the bear. I don't know if the couple brought an axe for chopping wood. I didn't find evidence of one in any of the reports. Some people react to seeing a bear by climbing a tree, but black bears are much better and faster climbers than us. Ray may have banged pots, shouted, or talked, but we don't know. Noises and words don't leave prints behind them.

A park publication called *The Raven* featured an article that said both victims "were killed by a single blow to the head." If the bear came crashing out of the brush, the powerful body of a large bear moving at speed would have been overwhelming. There would be no time for Ray to wonder about the species, assess the bear's intention, or plan a response. To be killed by a blow to the head is to be killed in an instant. The space between becoming aware of the bear and the first attack could have been less than the time it takes to blink. A bear the size of the one on Bates Island is strong and fast enough.

Given the condition of the bodies when discovered, it might have been difficult to determine whether Carola was killed instantly, but I prefer that version of events. The evidence seems to support it.

For Ray, however, the state of the campsite showed he knew what was happening. Undoubtedly, he was aware of the bear on the island. The evidence of his battle was left behind.

12.

BY MID-JUNE, FOUR MONTHS before the attack, the bear was spending his days looking for food, food, and more food. But soon, he started foraging less and roaming more widely. For a black bear, mating happens in the late spring.

In Ontario, the timing can range from mid-May through July. He worked his way along the edge of a pond. He found a half-dead fish caught in a beaver dam, a tangle of sticks and mud constructed by a beaver to make the water pool. He bit the fish in half and ate it, bones and all. No pride was lost in scavenging or stealing. It was a way to make it through leaner times. He flipped a rock, found grubs, and scooped them up.

That night, the bear curled into a ball near the root of a tree and slept deeply. Waking in the early morning, he found the day was warmer, each one longer, and the recent rain had turned the canopy a brilliant green. The leaves drank back the sun and shone like everything around him. The bear's coat was similarly gleaming. With food in better supply and the warm weather, he had shed the matted winter coat and replaced it with one of dense black. When he ran, it flashed and caught the light. His muscles were becoming even fuller and stronger.

And then he smelled something that made him a little dizzy.

We often think of dogs as having the gift of scent, but a bear's sense of smell is powerful too, perhaps as much as a hundred times more sensitive than a human's (although the power of the human nose is sometimes unappreciated).

Inside a bear's nose is the epithelium tissue, which lines the surface of his nasal cavity. It covers an area much larger than ours and has millions more scent-detecting nerve cells. A bear also has an olfactory bulb, which connects his nose to his brain to help manage incoming scents. His bulb is shaped like a tube and is five times larger than the one found in humans. The muscles that run through his snout are dexterous. They are sensitive, more like a human fingertip than the small nub that takes up space in the middle of our face.

All these tools mean the bear can detect human food or our bodies from up to twenty miles away. This is why the most common kind of bear encounter is a non-event. A bear can sense people in the distance. They avoid humans. Most of us have no idea when a bear is nearby.

If a person did catch sight of the bear that summer, he most likely caught their scent long before the person saw him. It would be rare for anyone to catch him off guard or by surprise. If they did, it might be because he was upwind of them. Many people put a bell on their backpack, clap, sing, or shout "Yo, bear" as they are hiking through thicker brush, walking beside a rushing river, or caught in the wind. These are not necessarily deterrents for a bear, but it would help him know people are close. In most cases, the bear will steer clear.

I went through Opeongo Lake that same summer, in 1991. The trip I led was a party of nine people and three canoes. There is safety in numbers. It was a large enough group that, unfortunately, we rarely saw wildlife. The sound of us coming came close to scaring every last bird away.

But the smell the bear caught at that moment wasn't food; it was something far more alluring. For us, with our comparatively dull noses, it's probably impossible to imagine how profoundly a bear's sense of smell must affect his sex life.

Up on his feet, the bear shook himself and set off in the direction of the scent. He walked in a straight line, not stopping to forage or nibble on branches. A male can lose up to 20 percent of his body weight during mating season, as they eat less. He went with a purpose; there was no mistaking the smell of a female. He recognized her. A good one. What happened next would depend on where in the reproductive cycle the bear found the female in.

Mother bears have a fearsome reputation, but this applies more to grizzly bears than black. Many people have first-hand experience of getting too close to cubs. When they do, the mother might woof, snort, paw the ground, or maybe, as a last resort, charge. She might swipe or bite if feeling particularly threatened.

A few years ago, a mother bear and her three cubs started hanging around an Algonquin Outfitters store. Jerry kept a close eye on the family, worried about the potential for conflict. At this store there was a campground and a restaurant. Around the back of the building was a grease container with a bear-proof lid on it. No matter how carefully they cleaned the container and the lid, the mother bear would circle around and give it a lick.

But as the mother made her rounds, she had her cubs walk in a wide arc around the campground to stay away from people. She watched the cubs closely. Jerry said it appeared as though she was showing them how to exercise caution. People could provide sources of food, but her message to her cubs was clear: *Stay away*. This is the most common reaction mother bears have toward people. They want to keep their distance.

A mother with cubs will also stay away from male bears. A study in Sweden found that, despite the danger, mothers will choose to live closer to humans, their other likely foes, during mating season in order to use our settlements as a shield, protection from the males. The internet is littered with clashes between large males and fierce mothers. When a male comes close, cubs are trained to run, climb trees, and scatter, anything to escape. There are documented instances of a male bear killing a cub that is not theirs. They do this, scientists think, because when a female has cubs, she is not fertile. If a mother loses her cubs, she will go into heat. That gives the male bear a chance to mate.

The bear scented a female who didn't have cubs. She was alone, though she lived in a range beside her sister. There are roughly two thousand black bears in Algonquin Park at any given time. The females tend to have smaller ranges, but they overlap in places with the males. She was ready to mate and had made excursions outside her territory to lay down a scent trail. It was no mistake that the male found her, but she remained cautious. For a while, she kept her distance from him, staying ahead and sniffing to check his mood.

There's evidence that bears remember each other and have favourites. Females have been seen to nuzzle and lightly bite a mate two months after the season is over.

The bear caught up to the female. Male black bears have been recorded making plaintive sounds when approaching a female, thought to be a way of communicating that he wants to make contact.

We don't know why one bear is attracted to another, but we humans do share with bears a similar central nervous system. We are both mammals. Blood runs through our veins and our hearts pump. It's hard to draw conclusions about bear behaviour based on human senses, but it might be equally as ridiculous to suggest that we could never understand anything about bears except for what we observe. Behaviourism is a school of thought that takes this to an extreme by only focusing on measuring observable behaviours. Frans de Waal, the author and primatologist, told a great joke about an overreliance on external cues: Two behaviourists have sex and afterwards one asks the other, "That was great for you. How was it for me?"

The bear's sensitive nose must play into his attraction. What the female bear ate recently might be close on her skin, hovering on her breath, even the patch of dandelions she munched on a few days ago—the scent still lingered around her. She ate so many of them, the golden heads popped into her mouth. They tasted like the sun. Now the light from them felt as though it ran through her ears and rested gently on her tongue.

Bears rub against trees. Probably to leave scent for others. The glands under her skin must have been hypnotic. Males follow females to assess receptiveness. They will sniff the ground in the place where a female had sat down. They will sniff the female directly when permitted.

The two bears travelled alongside each other for a while. They came to a patch of clover, which she loved to eat at that time of year. The flowers have their highest protein content and are easier to digest as their cell walls haven't developed as much cellulose and lignin, the structural materials of a plant. The two bears sat in the clump of clover and chewed, the sun to their backs, the sweet tickling their senses, not even allowing the persistent blackflies that buzzed around their ears to bother them.

After a day, a younger male found them. He was bold for his age. He had left his mother a year before and was in that late-teenage phase of testing the edges. The younger bear hung around for a while, trying to close the distance between himself and the female. The larger bear didn't seem bothered. He ignored the young one at first. Sexual maturity doesn't occur until three or four years of age, but a male is often not successful in mating until a few years after that.

Rather than getting the message that he wasn't being perceived as a challenger, the young bear felt hopeful. Maybe he had a chance. But the larger bear wasn't having it. He swiped once and huffed, which was all that was needed. The young bear took the point. He ran off.

If a larger male of a similar size and condition as the bear had made a play for the female, things would have been different. Males will fight for the right to mate. There have been battles that are so vicious they end in death. Many older male bears have scars around their neck and face.

With the rival dispatched, the two bears continued to travel together for about a week. The female knew the advantage of having a large male at her side. She had the chance to eat things that she otherwise might not get access to. They came across a nest of ant pupae. She took her time scooping them all up.

Soon after, the bear tried to mount the female. It took three tries, but he managed. They copulated for just under an hour. The male has a bone in his penis, a baculum. It may help with prolonged mating and placement. Also, it provides stimulation and encouragement for a female to ovulate.

In the final minutes, the male shook and shuddered, a series of fluttering thrusts that ended in ejaculation. Mating is believed to be exhausting for the male.

They stayed together for a while longer. Maybe the male stuck around to give his sperm time to fertilize her egg before another male had a chance. It was a good idea in this case as, soon, the female bear would decide to mate again.

When the female bear did wander off, she didn't become pregnant. While the fertilization was successful, the egg stayed in her uterus. The embryo, a blastocyst, wouldn't implant until she had dug into her den the next fall. By then, she would have gained enough weight and the egg could become embedded. On the other hand, if she were too thin, or unwell, the blastocyst would be reabsorbed into her body. This is a built-in form of birth control. A female may have cubs with more than one father in the same pregnancy.

After mating, the bear's mind turned back to food. He knew

of a special place. There, buckets poured out stuff like overcooked spaghetti with red sauce or the skin of baked beans. Sometimes there were bins that were filled with soggy potato chips, stale crackers, or a swipe of peanut butter stuck on a crust of toast. Plastic bags could be ripped open to reveal rubbery hot dogs or the rinds of mouldy pork chops. He wouldn't be alone there—the spot attracted other bears—but the risk of conflict with either bears or people was worth it.

Part Five

CLOSE ENCOUNTERS

13.

DAVE AND I WERE on a family road trip, heading home after visiting our family in Nova Scotia. With the two boys, we landed in a motel in New Brunswick. After a long drive and a dip in the swimming pool, the room resembled a crime scene, strewn with two wet boys, open suitcases, bathing suits, and hamburger wrappers. Dave had collapsed, belly up, on the bed. A teddy bear and my younger son, Max, sat in the middle of the mess.

I watched Ben wrestle his wet legs into a pair of sweatpants. It was an admirable effort, and once he was finished, I noticed the pant legs were too short. He had grown so much over that summer—he was now twelve years old—that the cuffs and his ankles had parted ways. I wondered if Dave would ever notice short pant legs. Doubtful. I had a thought, almost teasing myself, that I had to stay alive until the boys were full-sized or else their ankles would be forever exposed.

Max was almost the same age I had been when my dad told me he was dying. Max had large, round eyes, and when he asked me a question about the future, he would stare and breathe heavily until I gave him an answer. I wasn't only a mother; I was the source of everything certain. I had a new appreciation for how brave my dad had been to tell me he was dying while looking into his sweet child's face. It was a painful thought, hot and sore. I tried to avoid it.

I was about to take a hard-won shower when I turned to look in the mirror. There was a black spot on the back of my shoulder.

I wasn't entirely surprised. I have fair skin with blue eyes and blond hair, a complexion that means I have to be careful about sun exposure and wearing sunscreen. But for years I'd had my skin cleared at regular checks. When I talked to my doctors about risks, they placed emphasis on the environmental causes of cancer. Many genetic links have since been established, but the map of the human genome was only completed in 2003. Much of the research that has given us recent insights was just getting going. Cancer was more commonly discussed as something random. It was more a matter of luck. Sometimes it struck.

When we returned home, I made an appointment with my doctor, had the spot removed, and booked a follow-up about the results. I had published a novel the year before and was busy touring. I wasn't thinking about the significance of the appointment. It was one more item on a long list of things to do.

Fall had settled in. In Toronto, the sun sets early at that time of year, around 5 p.m. I went through the garden gate, and my boots crunched over the gravel and weeds of our parking spot behind the house. An alley runs along the back of the row of houses. Metal garage doors line the narrow road on either side. It feels private and quiet. A few brown leaves skipped across the pavement, and the afternoon wind swept around me. Someone had been prowling around with a spray can the night before. Fresh red paint slashed across the brick.

The clouds pressed down. It was chilly; I pulled my coat tighter, and the light flattened as I walked. The corners grew darker.

Every step I took drew me closer. *Tap*, *tap*, *tap*, the heels of my boots sounded on the cold pavement. I walked across a parking lot, waited at the traffic lights, and continued another block to the hospital. As I entered, the slight suction from the revolving door came as a pressure in my ears. The smell of disinfectant rose to greet me. I stood inside the hum of a large atrium. The elevator button lit up. I watched the numbers count down. The minutes were slipping away, but I wasn't aware of it. I didn't anticipate what was about to happen.

When I was young, I thought I'd stop having nightmares. I imagined growing up was supposed to be about leaving childhood fears behind. But now that I'm older, I know that it doesn't work that way. I'm still scared; it's just the things that terrify me have changed. My greatest fears no longer happen at night, when my eyes are closed. Instead, they happen in the light of day. When I am awake.

I was in a domestic phase of life. I had two kids, two cats, a dog, and a few more sad-looking plants. By that point, I had scaled mountains, climbed granite faces, lowered into crevasses in glaciers, skied volcanoes, and paddled into rivers full of frothy white water. I had dodged rocks and hitchhiked alone. I had gone into the wilderness for weeks by myself. I had bought an old van with worn brakes and driven her up steep mountain passes and made it back down. I had given birth to two babies, one of whom had an umbilical cord wrapped twice around his neck. All of us survived.

I had lived alongside a bear, stood close enough to mountain lions, and jumped over rattlesnakes. I'd shaken a few scorpions out of my shoes too.

Walking down the corridor toward my doctor's office, passing people who walked softly in thick-soled shoes, between walls coated in institutional yellow and baby-blue doors, the signs reminding me to wash my hands—I had no reason to feel that anything dramatic was about to happen.

I sat in a chair covered in vinyl. There was a flat-screen TV replaying a loop of news, a serial killer due in court, anti-poverty legislation, postal workers going on strike. I heard my name called and was surprised to see my doctor. She works in a teaching hospital and it's usually a resident who comes out to greet me.

"Oh, Diana," I said when I saw her.

Usually, I call her Dr. Toubassi out of respect for her education and how she's cared for my family. I corrected the slip, but she waved this away, not bothered with formalities.

Still, though, I caught a crackle, a small pop of static, between us.

The door hissed open. I followed her and we passed the nursing station. I waved hello to the nurses who had given my kids their vaccinations, taken out splinters, checked fevers, and tested suspected broken wrists. My family went there to be healed. They put us back together.

I sat in a chair in a small office, near an examination table with fresh paper pulled along its length. The fluorescent lights had a soft buzz. It wasn't dark. There was no rustling in the bushes, no dark shapes in the distance, no sound of a twig snapping under a soft foot.

Instead, Dr. Toubassi sat behind her computer. The screen flickered to life. Her straight expression lit up with my test results. "It's cancer," she said.

I left the office and started to cry in the waiting room. Another patient approached me and asked if I was okay. I told her I'd received some hard news. She rifled around in her purse for a tissue. This made the tears come harder. She found the package and offered me one. I've learned many things from having cancer. That first lesson was about the kindness of strangers.

When Dave came home, we went to my office. I have a reclining chair near the window. It's large and blue and has a footrest that pops out when I lean back. We sat in it together. I told him that I had the same cancer as my dad.

"How old was he when he died?" Dave asked for a reminder.

"Forty-two."

I was forty-five.

CANCER IS THE NAME for a collection of diseases, but it's characterized by abnormal cells that divide uncontrollably. They destroy the healthy tissue.

The words in Old English for cancer describe the disease as something like a snake bite or a scorpion sting rather than a systemic disorder. One example is *cancer-wund*, which is a wound made by an ulcerous sore, or canker. In other instances the word is *cancer-ald*, where *cancer* is combined with *ald*, which means a bite. Luke Demaitre writes about "the eating action" used to describe cancer in Old English and Latin. A biting disease.

Before he died, my dad had surgery that left a wound that travelled from his mid-back and twisted up through his armpit and onto his shoulder. The scar was large and angry and a last attempt to cut out cancer. My dad's incision was held shut by thick staples. My young mind attributed it to a dragon. This was the bite that I imagined had been left by a row of metal teeth.

DAVE AND I STARTED crying and held each other. Our bodies fit easily. When I'm sad, there's a place for my forehead in his neck. My shoulder tucks perfectly under his arm. He smells like home.

His longer breaths, and larger lungs, eventually slowed mine. We agreed we'd tell the kids that I had a weird spot and needed an operation. If the cancer had spread, the treatment would depend on the extent. It made sense to wait to tell them more once we had a clearer diagnosis and a plan.

Dave and I had moved through the world together for over twenty years by then, but the challenges had been external. We'd drawn a circle in the sand and decided to stand together inside it. Sometimes we faced each other in the circle. Sometimes we stood side by side. Especially since we'd had kids, I'd pictured us standing back to back. This was what a marriage meant to me. It was a place I could step inside and be safe. A decision. A configuration.

Once our tears had dried, Dave was the first to speak. "I always assumed we'd grow old together," he said.

There can be a false sense of security in being a human. My blue chair sat in a house made of brick. When the winds blew,

I didn't feel them. Soon it would snow and we'd stay warm inside the walls. The sun lowered and I summoned the light by flicking a switch. I could turn on a tap and watch clean water run. Our built environments feel so convincing, don't they?

But every now and then something happens. A reminder. The mask of control slips to the side and there is a glimpse of what lies behind. We are subject to natural forces. We are delicate, vulnerable creatures, no matter how much time we spend telling ourselves otherwise. Our teeth are blunt, our skin is thin, and our hearts flutter close to the surface. We are subject to the pull of the moon; we can be shifted by the tides and pushed by the wind. We burn under the sun.

Time, people, love, they are fleeting. We are born, grow, and move across the land until we pass by. The world is in a constant state of change. My life is no exception, even if, sometimes, or for a brief moment, I may have tricked myself into thinking otherwise.

14.

ON TUESDAY, OCTOBER 15, 1991, neither Ray nor Carola showed up for work.

This was the day after Thanksgiving weekend in Canada, about six weeks before the US holiday. The harvest comes earlier.

Canadian Thanksgiving is not such a big event as the American version. While it's tradition to celebrate with a meal, there isn't a set time to gather. Some people have a big Sunday dinner, while others will mark it on Monday. Increasingly, there is resistance to the holiday in acknowledgement of the country's poor record of holding up treaty agreements with First Nations, the legacy of residential schools, and an ongoing genocide. The colonial framework that was put in place when Canada became a dominion in 1867 continues to chew through the land and our relationships on it.

For many, this time of year is the start of things like leaf raking, turning on the furnace, and wearing thicker sweaters. Many people take a four-day weekend, which is why the couple weren't missed until Tuesday.

A phone rang in the offices of Algonquin Park. The buildings are low to the ground, made of wood with beams that blend into their surroundings. When the park isn't busy, the offices tend to have a hushed environment. Park staff wear soft-soled shoes and muted colours. Their business doesn't tend to be urgent. Many of the staff find jobs in the park because they love being outside. When they are in the administrative buildings, they have a look of patient yearning on their faces—there is a place they would rather be.

I imagine that morning, with the Thanksgiving weekend over, it was quiet. I can almost hear the mechanical ring of a land line, a lever against a bell, spill across the counter in a near-empty office.

When a member of the park staff picked up, the person on the other end of the line asked if anyone had seen the couple, or if they had checked in.

This kind of call to the park office wasn't unusual or alarming. In the 1990s, sometimes a party of backcountry campers decided to stay out an extra night. They didn't think of the people who might miss them back home. Sometimes a party had arrived home but forgot to let others know they were safe. Occasionally, a canoe dumped over, hit a rock, people got lost, or they miscalculated the number of miles they could cover every day. They came in after they had been expected, late but unharmed.

Now our land is mapped, tracked, and monitored by satellite. A map of every inch of ground can be called up on a computer. Few people become lost anymore, even if we might prefer it. Even some bears can no longer escape. A bear with a chip implanted or ear tags can't shake his tracking collar and disappear. He will be tracked until a battery dies down or he does. With technology, most of us live in a permanent state of being found.

In 1991, there were cellphones, but not the sort that could be carried in a pocket. There wasn't a way to send a quick text to tell your mom that nothing was wrong. A hand radio—it looked like a large walkie-talkie—worked in Algonquin Park if it was near one of the radio towers that stood around the edges, but much of the park didn't have reception. And most people, besides rangers, park staff, or those who worked at outfitting stores, didn't carry a radio. It was normal to be out of touch with your friends and family for days, or weeks, or months.

On rare occasions, when there wasn't an explanation for why people were missing, a phone call could spark a search. Usually, the people were found fairly quickly. A chain of phone calls to issue assurances went around. Everything tended to work out most of the time.

Now, a backcountry trip in Algonquin Park has to be booked five months in advance. The process includes giving the names of every member in the party and selecting the specific campsites you will stay at every night. Back then, many people communicated their routes using a less formal arrangement. They left a note tucked under the windshield wiper of their car.

I'm not sure how the couple left their route, but they were diligent. A few people have a hazy memory that they might have done this.

Jerry Schmanda and the others who were working at the store knew that the couple had put in their boat at Opeongo. The staff they rented from at Avery's also probably knew the couple's route, given that this used to be the content of most casual conversation. If not, it didn't take much detective work to figure out where to look. Their car was found locked in the upper parking lot.

An employee of the Algonquin Outfitters store, Chris, set out for the island to do a routine check to make sure the couple was okay. He was a junior employee that year.

Chris turned the key on the boat. A puff of gas from the motor found his nose, a scent many boaters associate with a sense of excitement. There is a kind of power in slowly steering the boat away from the shore, pressing the throttle, and watching the nose lift. When the boat rises to a faster speed, skipping across the waves can feel a little like flying. It was cold that morning, not more than six degrees Celsius. Chris probably pulled his jacket tighter and looked north across the large expanse of water.

Opeongo Lake is shaped like a body. There are two branches like arms at the top, one reaching slightly east and the other west. The outfitting store is near the toes at the south end. Bates Island lies in the southern third of the lake and spans the middle. There is a channel on either side. The island is about twenty-five acres in size. From overhead, it takes the shape of a crescent moon.

When I worked in Algonquin Park, we were told that camping on an island like Bates was one of the safest choices a camper could make. There was little chance of finding a black bear on an island because he would never feel cornered or trapped. If the bear heard people coming, his instincts would kick in. He would hop off the land, into the water, and swim away. It was an easy escape. This truth felt so irrefutable that I remember an open question among staff at our camp: If on an island, was it even necessary to secure your food? With hindsight, I realize that deer and moose sometimes choose to have a calf on an island. Berries grow on islands. Garbage can be left on islands. It follows that a bear might be on an island looking for food too.

Approaching the island from the south, as Chris was that morning, there is a channel around the island on the left, to the west. It's the route that motorboats take to navigate safely because it's deeper.

Jerry had driven the water taxi around that way many times during that long weekend. He took people out on fishing excursions, dropped off gear for a trip, and ferried canoes to save a party a long paddle up the length of the lake. He had glanced at the island a few times and remembers seeing the couple's boat pulled to the beach. The campsite they chose lay the farthest to the east. Their boat sat in the distance, but the glimmer of silver aluminum was visible. He didn't think the boat had moved during the weekend, which wasn't unusual. Many people spend their days on the campsite, swimming and fishing and cooking by the fire. Jerry didn't think anything of it.

Chris drove his boat up to the campsite. There is no dock, only rocks and sand that climb toward the land. It becomes shallow enough that the bow would grind against the pebbles of the thin strip of beach. The draw of a motorboat is too deep to get that close. Chris must have cut the motor, hopped out into knee-deep water or jumped to the shore, and held the bowline of the boat to pull it in a little farther.

Most backcountry campsites in Algonquin Park are marked with a bright-orange sign. They usually have a few spots where people have collectively decided to pitch their tents. There is also a designated place for a campfire. The ring of rocks is stacked in a circle to contain an open flame.

There is sometimes a sign that points to a box with a hole in the top, a makeshift bathroom. In the backcountry, outhouses usually don't have walls. There are as many names for them as people who have sat on them: throne, privy, treasure chest, shitter, bog, k.y.b.o. (keep your bowels open), latrine, biffy, or thunderbox. Whatever you call them, the exposure often comes with a spectacular view.

The bank of this campsite is held tight by interlacing roots that form a rough set of steps to climb up. Though the site is treed, it's easy to walk between them. White pine trees dominate, elegant, stately, almost regal. Their bark is rough and textured. If you put a hand to one, it's clear there is something wise inside. The trees stand firm, their feet planted deep, with roots bumping through the ground like knuckles. There are a few birch trees interspersed with the others, the bark peeled in curls around the trunk.

All around the campsite area, pine needles spread out like a carpet. They break underfoot and let out a heavy scent. The dirt underneath is pressed down tight and the brush is cleared in the main area. Through the summer, smaller branches get stripped by campers for kindling to start their campfires. The largest trees are left behind, standing in stark relief. Toward the back, small spruce and balsam make the bush thicker.

When Chris arrived, he stood near the front of the campsite. With a quick look, he could see that there wasn't anyone walking around. He noticed the tent was set up. The flap of the door was unzipped. He called out the couple's names and, almost immediately, felt a prickle of fear.

Chris picked up his radio and made a call back to the store.

He spoke out loud as he looked around the campsite. A few things seemed odd. A camping chair had been knocked over.

There was a bag of groceries in the boat. There was another near the beach. When the static of his voice came through the speaker at the other end, Jerry heard the alarm behind his words. Chris talked into the radio, wondering aloud if this was the scene of a murder, a double murder, or a suicide. He didn't know, but he did draw one conclusion that Jerry remembers clearly.

"Whatever happened here," Chris said into the radio, "it isn't natural."

15.

THAT JULY, THREE MONTHS before the attack, the bear kept travelling. He followed a similar route to the previous year, moving in a southward direction toward the special place that held sensory memories. He took small diversions for berries or fish when he felt the extra distance might be worth it. He spent much of his time dozing that summer, especially during the hottest parts of the day. He wasn't restless, because food was everywhere. He foraged at the cooler ends of the morning and night.

He visited the special place every July when the visitors started coming in large numbers to the park. He had learned long ago to avoid people, especially crowds, but there were times when it was worth the risk of getting closer. When he did, it was in search of human garbage. It's calorie-dense and, compared with hunting, much easier to get your teeth around. Garbage never fights back.

He headed toward an open-pit dump.

THE STUDY OF LARGE male black bears who lived around Algonquin Park in 1992 found that many of these bears had an efficient way of accessing human garbage. Most of the dumps were open pits back then. The large males tended to have one that they visited every year.

Stephen Herrero did a study of bears in Jasper National Park in 1968, when there was still an open dump in the park. He spent 750 hours over 141 days watching bears feed on garbage. During that time, over 7,500 tourists visited the dump to watch the bears. He saw hundreds of people approaching bears, "including 57 situations in which people threw rocks or chased bears." In all these interactions, a bear never struck, bit, or even touched a person. Herrero was astounded by the tolerance the bears showed, and by the humans' lack of caution. "It's a strange world where people can be like that with a large animal," he said.

It's also a strange world where a large animal can be this accommodating, especially one with sharp teeth and claws. Black bears have the capacity to be incredibly forgiving. It's easy to focus on the moments when something horrific happens and overlook all the times it doesn't.

WHEN THE BEAR WENT to the dump that summer, he was not alone. He knew the other bears. He communicated many things, not with words but with his size, his health, his gestures, scents, and sounds.

The other bears stood back and let him go first. They kept their distance.

The bear quickly found a pile of food thrown out from a restaurant. There were meat patties, chicken, buns, ketchup, and pickles. Underneath that was a heap of doughnuts that could no longer be sold as day-old. To him they weren't stale; they were soft and sweeter than berries. They were more like the honey he might scoop from the nook of a tree, but this time he didn't have to endure all the stinging bees that buzzed in his ears or tried to climb inside his soft nose. The few larvae were extra protein. The membranes of their bodies popped and released juice between his molars. He ate and ate.

Once the bear had eaten enough to take the edge off his hunger, the other bears slowly circled closer. He let them. They moved with caution around the edges of his vision, but they judged that he wouldn't attack or show aggression when his belly was full.

It's often assumed that bears are loners. "Except for females with cubs, black bears are solitary animals," says the website of the Massachusetts Audubon Society. "Black bears are typically solitary creatures, except for family (a female with cubs) groups," explains an article from the National Wildlife Federation. "They're typically solitary," says *National Geographic*. Many articles list exceptions to account for moments when they are seen together, such as a female with cubs, or a pair during the mating season.

Especially for the male bears, this image fits with the villainous image of a large predator. They roam the land alone, with sharp incisors. It also fits with the stories we tell about loners and rogues, whether people or bears. They sit outside the social order.

Black bears are large mammals. Their numbers depend on the quality and quantity of food in their habitat. Food availability will limit how many bears can live together in any given area. When I asked Stephen Herrero, after his years of research, what questions he still had about bears, he replied, "The social life of bears. How black bears relate to one another."

BEN KILHAM HAS STUDIED black bears in the woodlands of New Hampshire for almost thirty years. He started by taking in orphaned black bears and raising them. When they were old enough to fend for themselves, he released them. He's kept up a relationship with a few of them. Food runs interference in his relationship with bears. It's not possible to extrapolate all his learning to wild bears, but things he has learned through close observation point to something new. Rather than loners, the bears he's observed are incredibly social.

Kilham is especially close with a female named Squirty. He raised her as a cub and let her go, but she's stayed close. She tolerates him on most days. He's clear that their relationship is more like a contract rather than a friendship. A dog will bend his behaviour around a person, but this is not the case with a bear. Ben and Squirty have forged a relationship based on mutual expectations. She tolerates him for a time. In return, he gives her food. He has the scars on his knee to show for the times he's crossed her line. In his book *Out on a Limb*, Ben is crystal clear about the terms of their relationship. "I had to conform to her world, not she to mine."

Kilham's research is qualitative, not quantitative. He's dyslexic and believes this gives him a distinct advantage when working with wild animals. He doesn't start with preconceived notions that he's read in books, as other researchers might. "We look for meaning in other people's theories," he writes. "Even when those theories directly contradict what we can see with our own eyes."

Kilham starts with simple observations and works outwards. He has collected his observations gradually. Over time, he has built his experiences and tried to ground them in theories about the lives of bears. He has observed that the female bears who live near him maintain overlapping home ranges. They develop long-term relationships with the bears who live around them. They communicate with the males, sometimes using them for cover. When there is a potential conflict, often a female will ask a male to move on rather than compete or fight.

Bears build relationships with social contracts based on food. If a crop in their area fails, they call in favours from others to whom they were generous in previous years. Like humans, Kilham thinks the bears "share surplus resources in times of need outside conventional home ranges." Other experts might recast this idea of sharing as tolerating, but to Kilham, the bears sometimes survive by using co-operation techniques.

What Kilham sees after years of study is a highly evolved intelligence. He's heard the different tones. They use a "mm-mm-mm" when they want to appease him or reconcile, but much of their communication with each other is through their noses. They rub on trees and place their scent strategically. They eat a wide variety of food and can adapt to local conditions, which demands flexibility.

Kilham talks about how humans tend to set benchmarks for animal intelligence. If an ape uses a tool, then we test to see if another kind of animal will show intelligence by using a tool.

If they aren't able to use it, then we form the assumption that the second animal has lesser abilities. For years, it was thought that apes were the only other animals who use tools, but this was only because of how the tests were designed. This meant we missed all the other tool users out there, like crows, dolphins, otters, elephants, and many others.

"We need to look harder," Kilham says.

He's observed how a sub-adult bear will follow behind a larger male, as if tracking or shadowing the movements. Kilham has caught this on camera, a male passing by, followed later by a sub-adult. It may be a way of learning from example. Burt, a male black bear, comes to spend time with Squirty, the female, on occasion. They will live side by side and forage together. He's seen larger males act as "bodyguards" to foraging females, allowing them access to food they otherwise might not get.

Social skills, and living with others, require intelligence. Jennifer Vonk, a comparative psychologist who studies animal cognition, has taught black bears to use a touch screen device. They could distinguish between pictures of a bear and a human. She's found evidence that they can be trained to count. They learned the skills she taught them faster than apes such as chimps and gorillas. "They were the most rapid learners," Vonk told author Gloria Dickie in her book *Eight Bears*. "Bears have outperformed the great apes I've worked with on many tasks."

When Vonk gave bears puzzle boxes with food inside, the bears showed an ability to test a hypothesis and reason. They continued to work on the task longer than cats. As I read about this research, I couldn't help but think of the peanut butter sandwiches that had been expertly extracted from my Tupperware.

At the dump, the bears had complicated relationships. They recognized and knew each other. Every encounter between them held their history, previous fights, peace agreements, and chances for food and to mate. If they meet for the first time, an order will be established between them.

THE BEAR SLIPPED THROUGH the chain-link fence and started to scavenge for garbage. He raised his head to sniff the scents of the females. Some had cubs that belonged to him. A few of the larger males had attacked and killed cubs, but at that moment there was no tension. Meat patties were far more important. Like most wild animals, if food is abundant and there is no threat, a bear will usually avoid conflict.

The bear fed well at the dump. He stayed until his body fat stores were replenished. By August, he was proud and his gait had a more leisurely roll about the hips.

As the older bear travelled farther away from the dump, a younger male tracked behind him for about half a day. The young one learned from tagging along, things like the good spots for the seasonal berries and where the sun catches the bush on the edge of a meadow. He learned about knocking over stumps in low-lying valleys, the insects hiding inside sent running in all directions. There were grasses and leaves and nuts to eat along the way. These lower-calorie snacks can feed a bear well, but it takes time and effort to get enough of them.

A black bear can eat up to thirty thousand blueberries a day when they are in season. The lasting effects of this feast don't only end with a full stomach. Bear scat is often speckled with seeds. A bear eats and then wanders, meaning there are many berry patches that are a result of a bear "seeding" the area. This new crop, in turn, might attract birds to the area. A bear influences their habitat.

When food is abundant, bears tend to follow their established patterns. When crops fail, and key parts of their diet are missing, they will change their behaviour. As Jeremy Inglis told me, "If bears don't have enough natural food, if they don't have enough berries or nuts, or whatever they are feeding on, they will seek out those calories."

If berries are having a bad year because of a drought, the bear will find a replacement. A lack of food will disturb movements and patterns. Sometimes that will lead to conflict with humans.

In 1991, there was speculation that a shortage of food might explain what happened on Bates Island. After the attack, however, when the bear was examined during a necropsy, they found that he was in good condition. He had ample stores of fat. There is no evidence that his way of life was disrupted by shortage or drought.

There was also speculation that the bear was sick in some way. The head was cut off and sent for testing to see if there was a biological explanation for the bear's behaviour. When the results of the necropsy came back, it was found that the bear had "absolutely no significant health problems." His eyesight was good. No broken teeth. No arthritis. No evidence of prior injuries other than what would be usual for a bear of his age. There were no lesions or wounds besides those he received when he was shot.

This bear wasn't starving—just the opposite. His size, age, and health showed his good condition. He was one of the most successful bears around.

Part Six

DEFENCE vs. OFFENCE

16.

I WAS DIAGNOSED WITH three instances of melanoma. During an operation, a surgeon cut in four places, taking a wide margin around the cancer, like a border for defence. This left thirty-four stitches in my back. The skin on my shoulder was pulled together tight enough to pucker. There was a smaller slice from my throat, a spot in the process of changing.

When I came home, the bandages were soaked through with blood. Dave helped me remove them.

After being given instructions by a nurse, Dave prepared to remove my stitches too. He used tweezers to pick up the first stitch. He warned that he would have to tug to loosen it enough to slide the bottom blade of the scissors underneath it. My skin was primed and ready to protest when anything came near it. I let out an involuntary sound, half moaning, half gasping. All around the cut, the nerves stood up.

To cut the first stitch, Dave pushed the scissors under the stitch. He snipped. There was a pull of pain. And then a release. I felt the thread of the stitch wind out of its hole. I was so glad to have these scratchy, tight things out of me. Except it hurt. I didn't want to show Dave how much. And we had many more to go.

Battle-sweat, a kenning for blood.

I received the news that, as far as the doctor could tell, the cancer hadn't spread, but a blood test identified a genetic mutation. My CDKN2A gene is faulty, which means a protein that acts as a tumour suppressor fails to activate.

In our first meeting, my dermatologist picked up on my tendency to google. He asked if I knew about the survival rates for people with melanoma. I had them memorized and liked the odds. I rattled them off. At my stage, more than 95 percent of people with melanoma were still alive after five years.

He shook his head. "None of those statistics apply to you."

My condition is rare. The studies are few. I found a research paper with a small sample size. It shows that by the age of fifty, only 38 percent of people with my mutation are cancer-free. After that age, a graph shows how we start falling down what looks to me like a staircase of death. These numbers may, or may not, bear out in me, but I've had many biopsies since my first operation.

While discussing the mutation in a meeting with my surgeon, Dr. Reedjik, I talked about my outdoor adventures. Like many people with cancer, I wondered if I had done something to bring it on. He thought the time I'd spent outdoors, canoeing on lakes, travelling across glaciers, and climbing in deserts, didn't help. But given the location of the melanoma, it was more likely that genetics would dictate the course of my disease.

There was one thing I could do, however, that might influence my fate. "For you," the surgeon said, "the ideal exposure to UV light is none."

Even on a cloudy day or in a northern climate, the UV radiation in sunlight can damage DNA. The mutation meant that I lacked natural protection. I asked Dr. Reedjik how, short of becoming nocturnal, I could avoid UV light.

"It's impossible," he said. "But you have to aim in that direction."

My terror mixed with a glimpse of early death. Old feelings came surging back, but this time the life I grieved was mine.

I had learned to cope with difficult things in a certain way. My ability to weather the elements in the wilderness, which by its very nature includes sun exposure, had helped me find strength, courage, and perspective. My first instinct after learning I had cancer was to get in a canoe and paddle away. Now, the way I'd learned to heal was the one thing I could no longer safely do.

And as I tried to imagine this new reality, one where I wasn't spending days on end out in the wild, another thing occurred to me. Friends send me stories of their bear encounters and forward me articles when a bear makes the news. I've not so quietly been convinced I'd go up against a bear one day. I was always getting ready, noticing a good stick I could grab to fight, making sure I had pepper spray, or planning my route back to the car. When camping, I'd tell people I was with, only half joking, "If a bear comes, don't worry. I've got this."

It was only now that I realized how foolish I was. I'd been preparing to fight a bear when the thing that would most likely kill me—my own DNA—had been lurking in a place much closer.

With the stitches out, my wounds were still raw. I started spending time in my office. Sitting in my recliner, I could wedge pillows around my incisions. I tried to write fiction, something I've done every morning for years, but I couldn't do it. Staring at a blank page of my notebook, I wondered where I had ever found the courage.

I started to suspect that when Dr. Reedjik had taken out the cancer, by accident he had also cut out my imagination.

At a loss, I found myself looking at a copy of my novel *The Bear*. I don't tend to look back on what I've written before, but I picked this object up because it felt estranged. I didn't recognize the author. Who wrote this? It felt like looking through old photos from another time, a different place, someone else's life.

When I wrote *The Bear*, I worked from my memory. It's pure fiction, an interpretation of what happened at Bates Island filtered through having kids of my own. The story has a relationship to the truth in the same way an expressionist painting might depict reality.

At the beginning of my novel, I'd included a brief author's note about the real-life circumstances I drew from. To my eye, the true story was recognizable inside my made-up version. For the families and the curious, I wanted to draw a clear line between fact and fiction. The note was my way of ensuring there wouldn't be any confusion.

As I sat in my blue recliner, I skimmed this note. I noticed a detail in what was found at the campsite on Bates Island. "A broken oar," I had written.

There was something wrong, but I couldn't quite place it. I stood up, stiff, having to move carefully because the long slashes on my back were still healing, and shuffled over to where I keep my old notebooks. Inside one of them, I found a newspaper article about the Bates Island attack. I reread it. It said a broken paddle was found at the campsite, which is what I remembered. So why, in the author's note, did I write "oar"?

It was frustrating to think I'd made this mistake, especially as I could no longer write. I had never healed from surgery before. I assumed I would never be able to write a novel again.

It drove me crazy to think that I had got this one thing wrong. I was weak, my muscles had been cut. I was prone to bursting out crying for barely perceptible reasons. I hadn't worn more than pyjamas by that point, but I found a reason to get out of bed. I started with the intention of answering that one question—paddle or oar?

Soon, I found more inconsistencies in the articles about the Bates Island attack. And in the novel, I had described the bear as "a rogue." What did that mean? Many bear experts disapprove of the term. I wondered if I knew anything at all.

Maybe I couldn't write fiction, but at least I could correct my past mistakes.

When I woke up at 3 a.m., I didn't wonder if my cancer had spread. Instead, I started looking for the contact details of people in the search party. I grabbed a yellow Post-it and jotted down all the things an oar would change about the attack. If the couple had paddled to the island, how long would the trip take? I couldn't remember from my trips. Given the time of year and the cold, had the couple left the dock dangerously late? Or had they arrived before sunset?

Every hour became urgent. By that time, I had lived three years longer than my dad. This felt like borrowed time. I made a list of questions. I was sore and tired. I suspected I might be dying, but finding answers became more pressing than fear.

I couldn't lift my left arm above my head, walk very far, or sit long enough to write, but I planned a canoe trip into the backcountry of Algonquin Park. I wanted to time how long it took to paddle to the island. I hoped to recreate the conditions the couple had been in. I wasn't supposed to go in the sun, but I figured I could manage it. A visit to the park in similar conditions would be the definitive way to settle any remaining questions. I secured a permit for Thanksgiving weekend, Friday, October 11, 2019. This was a date when I hoped to meet back up with my old self again.

By July of that year, I had interviews scheduled, archives to pick through, and campsites to visit. I ended up heading to Algonquin Park three times during my investigation, but this visit in July was my first drive alone after my operation. I found a way to sit in the driver's seat comfortably, which involved wedging a pillow and adjusting the seat.

By then, the scars on my back had a life of their own. They were prone to talking loudly and complaining when I did something they didn't like. The muscles around them tired quickly. My energy was low. My appetite was weak. I often lay down for a quick nap only to wake up two hours later feeling as though I'd been transported to another planet.

The first step of the journey, getting into the car, wasn't easy. Dave helped me in, tucking the pillow in around my back, placing a bottle of water in the cupholder, dropping a sunproof shirt on the seat beside me, and putting snacks within reach. He had packed a cooler with my favourite foods so I'd remember to eat.

I lowered the window, foot on the brake, suddenly unsure about what I was doing.

"Do you think this is a bad idea?" I asked him.

"Yes," he said with absolute confidence. He leaned through the window to kiss me on the lips and stood back. "And I can't wait to hear what you find out."

I started driving. I went north. Algonquin Park had helped heal me once before. I hoped it could help me again.

Part Seven

FINDING A CACHE

17.

THERE'S A SMALL ROOM with a fireproof door that sits under the visitor centre in Algonquin Park. It's quiet, an archive. Artifacts line the shelves, an old iron pot, forestry tools that look like forceps, and a pair of leather boots with the soles peeling off. I was the only one inside the room.

There is a library next door with articles from journals, books on wildlife, and hundreds of newspaper clippings. Apart from one aging computer, many documents stored in the archives aren't connected to the outside world. It felt like walking into the past, a place that existed in its own timeline.

After a few hours of digging, I found a binder with a photo of the Bates Island bear inside. Before I laid eyes on it, I didn't know that seeing a photo would be important. It was only while looking at the photo that I realized the bear had still felt imaginary to me.

Jeremy Inglis, the wildlife biologist, is based in Pembroke, Ontario. I'd been to his office the day before. It has yellow walls, fluorescent lights, and a panelled ceiling, all made to feel homey with a mix of skulls, bones, maps, radio collars, and a taxidermy bear standing over the desk. I'd told him a little about my project over email. He had made a considered decision about whether to grant an interview. Black bears get enough bad press. At the start of our meeting he asked, would the bear in my story be treated like “a demon”?

While looking at the photo of the bear, I considered Jeremy’s question more carefully. In many ways, the bear *had* become a dark, shadowy figure, an expression of my fear, rather than a being in his own right. The photo helped me understand something that should have been obvious: this bear had a life of his own.

The bear was dead in the photo. He lay on his side. There was a rope around his neck and paws. His eyes were closed, as was his mouth, but slack lips allowed for his teeth to show. His right paw was lifted close to his snout and I was struck by its size. The claws grew out from the fur of his foot, more like a dog than talons on a dragon. His black coat was glossy and full. He looked healthy.

He was different from the bears I’ve met in the wild. His expression was gone, but there was something else about him. When it comes to large predators, we observe one individual and tend to apply that behaviour across the species. This approach is far too generic.

Even my sons who are genetically similar will, when faced with the same situation, make completely different choices. I understand differences when it comes to dogs. I don’t expect the cattle dog or the collie I grew up with to make the same choices as the dog I live with now, a retriever. I have developed a few lasting friendships with horses. I allow them a personality.

I started to understand something that a few bear experts had mentioned: every bear has a distinct personality. In the photo, the bear was positioned in a similar way to how my dog, Phoebe, lies on her side. Phoebe is completely relaxed around people. She's been domesticated and bred to accommodate human lives (though, more correctly, we accommodate hers). I have had many chances to observe her. I've tried to understand her world view.

Though Phoebe can't speak or tell me stories, sometimes it feels as if there is a shared reality that forms between us. Sometimes I lie beside her and put my head on her shoulder. Our bodies are different, mine is smooth, hers is furry, but we have similar lungs and nervous systems. We breathe and sigh together. We live in the same house alongside each other. The afternoon sun comes through the window, a swirl of dust dancing in the beam. We both watch it. We aren't having a conversation, but sometimes I wonder if that removes a barrier. Nothing needs to be said or noted or discussed between us. We can just be.

For a moment, I could imagine putting my head on the bear's shoulder, the same way I do with my dog. I could close my eyes and hear him exhale. His body would be strong and warm under my ear. Fur coarser, muscles denser, but still breathing like me. Through the safety of the photo, I found a level of appreciation for the bear.

But any parallel I draw between my dog and the bear is wrong-headed. The bear was more than three times Phoebe's size. Phoebe is tame and her kind have been living with humans for thousands of years. A wild animal is guarded.

Another crucial difference between my dog and the bear in the photo: my dog is alive, not dead, and didn't spend the last five days of her life feasting on human remains.

It didn't take long, looking at that photo, to understand everything else I had wrong.

For years I'd focused my attention around people as the main characters in the story of the Bates Island attack. I've thought about the events from the perspective of the couple, or the search party, or my own reaction to the tragedy. I've tried to wrestle with what happened, but as my curiosity grew, my thinking had become circular. I'd gone around the same obsessions for twenty-eight years by that point, with different theories and new details, but I'd been chasing my own tail.

As I looked at the photo, I understood that my focus on the people involved had blotted out a larger set of questions. The stories I grew up with have a beating heart. They often centre on one character. Beowulf is one example. A hero. The action, details, empathy, and struggle, they all bend around him. The tale shows the force of individual characteristics and how, in the end, one man changes everything. Beowulf saved his people from the fire-breathing dragon. Much of the history I've learned, as a person with European ancestry, is plotted in this shape.

In Toni Morrison's essay about *Beowulf*, she makes the point that nowhere in the story do people ask questions about why Grendel was hell-bent on eating them. "Why had he placed them on his menu?" she writes. Grendel doesn't have a motive in the story. No one has tried to invade his home or stolen something from him. He's not a flesh-eater because he's hungry, seeking vengeance, or trying to settle a score. In the poem, he is evil, and other than that, he was, according to Morrison, "beyond comprehension, unfathomable" to the people he terrorized.

How many times had I read or told the story of *Beowulf* and never questioned the source of Grendel's trouble?

When I followed Morrison's thought, I understood that the bear wasn't beyond comprehension. I'd been hearing from the experts how bears are an intelligent species. They are individuals. They do individual things. And this bear switched from being wary of people, or cautious, or curious, and made an unusual kind of judgment. His personality altered what came after. If I wanted to understand why he attacked, I needed to know the motivations for his decision. I needed to understand this bear on his terms, not mine.

Was that even possible? It felt like trying to reach out and touch Grendel. I doubted I could do it, but as I held that photo, I knew I had to try.

18.

A RADIO TOWER LOOMED on the mainland, just east of Bates Island. When Chris pulled up to the island, he knew something was wrong. When he made a radio call to Jerry, the nearby tower picked it up. It sent the sound of Chris's voice over the wires and into the office of the Ontario Provincial Police.

Whitney is the first town that lies beyond the east gate of Algonquin Park. The office of the Ontario Provincial Police sits in a low-slung brick building just off Highway 60. Back then, the Whitney detachment, the local unit, monitored the radio waves on occasion. The officer who was listening caught the alarm in Chris's voice. They heard him speculate about the scene he found on the island, how he didn't know but it could be a murder, double murder, or murder-suicide. Though he was a junior employee at an outfitter and untrained as a first responder, Chris's speculation made sense to the police. It was much more statistically likely than what actually took place.

Rick Stronks, the chief park naturalist of Algonquin Park, explained how emergency services function in the park. When we met, he was friendly and generous with his time, but he didn't laugh easily.

Soon, he explained his unease. It was the day before a busy summer long weekend. He explained how the number of people inside the park would swell by ten thousand. He was responsible for everything and everyone that fell inside the borders. It was hard to know what the weekend had in store for him. Despite the strain, he had a playful quality. While he felt a great responsibility to the people in the park, his heart seemed to belong to the animals. His face became animated when discussing the other patrons in his domain: the bears, wolves, moose, and yellow-bellied sapsuckers.

In the high summer, the park operates more like a town than a wilderness area, but they don't have a police force, ambulance service, or hospital. They have to call all services in. And between the time of the call and the arrival of emergency personnel, there is often a long pause. Depending on where the accident has happened, it can take up to an hour or more for first responders to arrive. In the backcountry, response times can be much longer. It's up to the park staff to fill the void in between. That means employees are often responding to situations that lie far beyond their training, much like the one Chris found himself in that morning.

The police called the outfitting store to make contact. They agreed to meet at the store and return to the island together. That was how Officer David Stott and his partner, Steve Swrjeski, joined the search party. Others gathered, including a wildlife official from the park named Dan Strickland. They climbed into the boats and set off across the lake.

The leaves were probably at, or just past, peak colour. In fall, chlorophyll—the green pigment found in leaves that captures energy from the sun—is absorbed on deciduous trees. The yellow, orange, and red pigments were in the leaves all along, but when the chlorophyll fades, they are unmasked. The shortened day, or lack of light, triggers the tree to shed leaves. Soon, bared branches would claw at the sky, but on that day there must have been a stunning scene around the boat. The evergreens were interspersed with the changing leaves along either side of the lake.

No one I interviewed remembers the weather that day. They didn't mention the changing leaves, the colour, or the temperature. A harrowing event can turn the mind inward. When someone tries to tell a story about the past, they have to pick and choose between all the things that might have happened. Any detail the brain selects to focus on while telling a story will become a more prominent feature of a memory. Repeating that detail might influence the next retelling. Some events can blot out others. And experiencing the imprint of trauma changes the memories that come after. Memory is tricky.

The men in the boat, whether they stood in silence or engaged in friendly banter, probably had their eyes fixed forward. After the boat eased out from the dock and into the narrower channel, the water spread out on either side. The route to the island hooks to the right. Soon enough, Bates Island came into view.

At first, it would have looked as if the boat was headed for the mainland ahead. The island stretches out wide enough to create the appearance of a false north bank. But with a little more distance gained, it's possible to see the edges of the channel on either side. I'm sure a few of the men stared at its shape for clues, wanting to notice a movement or anything unusual. Birds often provide the best information. If there is carrion, or a carcass, the ravens or vultures will be the first to know about it. They can often be spotted circling above a kill, waiting for the right chance to get in.

While a few of the men may have checked out, staring at their hands or watching the water, others may have tried to imagine the range of things they might find on the island. Curiosity is a tool for survival. Exploring the possibilities would help them prepare for different scenarios. A little added fear can help focus the mind on what lies ahead too.

When I searched for the police officers who had worked on this case, I found an obituary first. Steve Swrjeski, the officer who shot the bear, had passed away more than ten years earlier. I found his partner's name, Officer David Stott, in a database of old newspaper articles. He was on the boat when the search party approached the island. To him, there was no doubt that something was wrong when they arrived. "It looked like a crime scene," he recalled.

In the summer of 2019, Dave agreed to an interview and invited me to his house. He lives on the edge of a small town about an hour east of Algonquin Park. When I pulled up, it was tidy. The details were what impressed me, the edge of the grass straight, the stone path swept, and the car pulled into the garage rather than left outside.

Dave's wife, Cheryll, greeted me at the door. She held a copy of my novel, *The Bear*, which had been published five years before. It's a novel that pulses with fear. The cover shows two children running hand in hand. Seeing the cover image reminded me of the strength of my obsessions. I didn't have the energy to fuel that kind of fear anymore. I walked into their living room ready to find answers. I hoped the facts would help me lay my fear to rest.

Dave was in the police force for more than thirty years. I started down my list of questions. They were things I'd read or heard that I wanted to confirm. His answers were crisp. I was astounded by his memory—the brand of the stove, the state of the pan, and the length of a boat. A few times he mentioned wishing he had his notes. He recalled things with such clarity that I imagined the details were etched across his brain. I asked Dave how he was able to remember.

"It was traumatic," he said, face blank, tone matter-of-fact.

When he said this, his expression didn't change. I realized that he was able to maintain a professional composure that I was sorely lacking. In the Stotts' living room, I kept tearing up at odd times while explaining the reasons for my investigation. I put my hand on my chest to steady myself as I talked. I searched too hard for the right word when silence might have been better, but then I left awkward gaps in the conversation.

In contrast, Dave was calm, accepting, observant, and precise. He was the type of person who reads more into body language than what someone says. I suspected he must have acquired the ability to hide what he was thinking, or hold back, while on the job. It was hard to read him. I admired his way of going about things. It struck me that we came at trying to find the truth from completely different directions.

When I write fiction, I focus on the emotion behind the story first. I feel the texture and the shape and fill in the details from there. Truth becomes something that I work toward. Lauren Groff, in her novel *Fates and Furies*, crystallizes the thought: "Fiction is the craft of telling truth through lies."

Dave worked in the opposite direction. He explained how he had learned to develop a theory of a crime. It's a process guided by clues and hard evidence. He didn't allow himself to be carried away by grand theories or stories. He checked his assumptions. He started with what was left behind, the aftermath, and figured out how to fit the pieces together. He linked them to construct the story.

I asked Dave if he gave any weight to other theories I'd heard about the attack over the years. There were some who speculated that it may have been a murder or suicide, or a combination of the two. It was such unusual behaviour for a black bear that some people believed the bear must have come to scavenge at the campsite later.

Dave gave me an emphatic no. The evidence had told him what happened at Bates Island. "It was all there," he said.

It didn't look as though the couple had spent a night on the island. This was supported by the coroner, who placed their time of death on Friday night. Dave remembers seeing brown paper grocery bags in the boat, as if someone had been carrying them up but never had the chance to finish the job. He talked about a few things that were new to me, like how there was gas found on the hide of the bear.

"Was there anything else on the beach?" I asked.

"A broken oar," he said.

Later, I confirmed this in the police report. It was in a typed note, confirmation that an oar, not a paddle, was found on the campsite. I wasn't the only one confused. On the necropsy, the autopsy of the bear, dated October 21, 1991, the pathologist identified the bear as "in connection with the death of 2 canoe trippers."

Up the bank, the tent was set up beside a large pine tree near the front of the campsite. The sleeping bags were inside the tent. Dave remembered they were still wrapped in green garbage bags. The ring of rocks marked the spot for the campfire. The two camping chairs were near the fire, one knocked over. The stove that sat by the cooking area was made by Coleman. Something had been cooking; there was still fat or oil in the bottom of the pan. There was a pile of firewood that had been collected and left beside the campfire ring. There was one small difference in Dave's memory: the Styrofoam tray of ground beef was unwrapped. Jerry had remembered it wrapped. Either way, they both considered it untouched.

The men did a quick search in case there was someone alive who needed immediate help. No one answered their calls.

Soon after, Steve Swrjeski, the officer with the Ontario Provincial Police, heard the sound. A huff. Steve was a hunter and an outdoorsman. It's not unusual, during hunting season, for people and bears to come into conflict over a carcass. Either a hunting party will come across one and startle the bear who's made a kill, or if a human has a kill, a bear might want to check if he can wrestle his way in. By necessity, a hunter and their prey will get to know each other's habits. Often, their knowledge of each other's ways can be far more intimate.

Charles Foster, a natural historian, wrote of his experience while hunting a stag. In order to make a kill, he had to see the world as his prey did. He tried to move into their state of mind, observed how they travelled over the land, tested for weakness, and watched for courage or fear. It's risk assessment. A good hunter tries to know the mind of the other. "It sometimes feels as if you've got two nervous systems running ecstatically in parallel," says Foster. "Yours and the stalked stag's."

Steve knew there was a bear on the island with them. He understood that black bears were timid, smaller than grizzlies, and usually shy around people. This bear didn't run off the back of the island and swim away. Instead, the bear hid, staying low, likely crouched and concealed by the thicker brush up the slope. When a boat full of men approached the island, the bear stayed.

And from the noises the bear made, he was feeling threatened. All Steve had with him was a .38 revolver. It wouldn't be enough.

The men were ordered back to the boat.

Though Steve wouldn't know more specifics, he would realize that for a black bear to stay put with that many people on the island, he must have a reason. He might be guarding a cache of meat.

The bear would want to keep it.

19.

IT WAS LATE AUGUST, early evening, less than two months before the attack. The bear stayed low to the ground with the thinner skin of his belly pressed to the earth. The last hour of sunlight sent an orange blush across the foliage. The earth had sucked back most of the puddles from the recent rain, but the soil remained moist and springy. Despite the warm day, there were still nice patches in the shadows. Where the leaves spread out and protected the ground, it was cool.

The bear had moved downwind. His ears were perched forward, curious, and he lingered in the brush, under cover of the leaves, to watch the coyotes for a moment. They hadn't sensed him yet, too consumed by chewing.

Ninety percent of the bear's diet was vegetation. He spent most of his time foraging, eating berries, maybe acorns or roots. It was pleasant to spend evenings eating and lounging at his leisure. But the chances he had to eat meat took a more prominent position in his mind. Any time meat was present, it came with risk. He had to stay alert. It occupied his full attention.

The bear had no doubt the carcass was his to take from the

coyotes, but he measured the situation first. Specifically, he wanted to make sure he knew how many other animals were present. He could see and smell three, but they lived in a pack. The others would probably be close by.

Whereas a human might have to take a moment to tell the difference between a coyote and a wolf by looking at size and characteristics, the bear knew with one quick sniff. He recognized the sharp stink from miles away. When he caught a stream of deer blood mixed in, he became interested. The way the two smelled mixed together had caught his attention, even though the coyotes attempted to blot it out with their stenches. Their urine, saliva, and rectal glands were active. They lifted their legs to squirt scent on everything around the land, as if that gave them rights.

The bear was impatient. Minor creatures like coyotes didn't deserve this much time with a carcass. They were smaller and needed less meat, and even if he hadn't come across it first, any meat was his to take. After he was finished, there would be plenty for the coyotes to pick at with their small jaws and pointed teeth. They liked to crack the bones and eat the marrow. They could lick the joints and eat the larvae laid by the flies. That was more than enough to sustain them.

What gave the bear pause, the reason he watched longer than he might have otherwise, was the whiff on the wind. There had been a loud crack in the distance when he was miles away. The residue of gunpowder still hung in a fine cloud. It landed on his tongue. It clung to his gums. It had a chalky taste.

The bear had scented people and knew the direction from which they had walked in a few hours before. It wasn't hard to track them. They were never subtle. They yodelled their sounds and cackled loudly from their throats. He had stayed far away, but often they appeared like a kind of stain on the landscape. They wore bright markings, orange vests that looked like a poisonous flower. They had wide feet that clunked on the ground like hooves and smelled of rubber soles and chemicals. Their breath carried a sourness that lined their stomachs, the odour of their fear.

The coyotes were prone to taking more risks around people. They often went closer. This didn't mean the coyotes were braver or bolder than the bear. It had to do with their numbers and their higher reproduction rate. And that they were smaller and slinky. Harder for a human to hit the target.

The coyotes, like the bear, had tracked the progress of the people throughout the day. They had come on the trail, over the ridge, and moved to the edges of the open meadow. The deer had been plucking the heads off the great bloom of wildflowers.

When the bear heard the shot, he caught a whiff of blood pouring like a river of scent down the ridge. He licked his lips.

Hunters had shot the deer, but the bullet hadn't landed exactly as they intended. It pierced the muscle to the side of her heart. Instead of dropping, the deer was able to bolt. She ran into the brush and through the trees for cover.

The men tracked the deer for a long time. They followed the trail of blood, small splatters on leaves, a splotch on a rock, and a dribble across a fallen log. When it started to rain, the men lost the blood trail. Eventually, they had to admit defeat. They turned to head for home.

The deer kept going for as long as she could. Eventually, the blood loss was too much. She found a safe place to hide and died in the brush. Her carcass left a large meal, a surprise, that would be consumed by different animals.

The warm night allowed a batch of mosquitoes to hatch and flourish in a puddle. With the light lowering, they came out from under the leaves where they'd been sheltering. They couldn't get through the bear's tough hide, but they liked to hone in on his most sensitive parts—the thinner fuzz that held his testicles, around his nose, and where the veins traced the surface inside his ears. When they found him, the high-pitched buzzing came in a cloud.

The bear twitched an ear in irritation. That movement was small and subtle, but the tip of the bear's ear touched a leaf. This leaf fluttered in the peripheral vision of one of the coyotes. She was a twitchy thing with a highly strung nervous system. She tensed, which caught the immediate attention of her companions. For a moment they had been consumed by their good luck. There is danger in being too focused on food. They all stopped what they were doing, noses to the wind, and waited.

The bear saw this and knew the game was up. He lifted his large body. He put a single paw forward. A twig snapped.

The coyotes splayed their front legs to brace. If the wind had been coming in the other direction, they would have known there was a bear from miles away. But this bear had snuck up. One coyote let out a yip. They lowered their snouts and darted off.

They wouldn't go far. They'd wait around at an acceptable distance. If anything, they were welcome. They would alert the bear if any other animal was approaching. They became like an advance warning system.

The men with their metallic-tasting bullets had done the hard work. It was a rare chance to chew on protein after expending relatively little energy to get it. All gain. Eating that carcass was close to a kind of ecstasy, the blood flowing over his powerful teeth and slipping down his throat. The comfort of a full stomach, the warmth glowed from him.

Much of the meat a bear eats will be scavenged. Carrion, the decaying meat on a carcass, might melt out from the snow. If it's been bug-infested, so much the better: that means more nutrients.

The bear ate and ate.

With his middle heavy, he was feeling lazy, slower; all the food was busy moving around inside him. It was breaking down, finding its way into his bloodstream, and making him dozy. The night had lowered all around.

He made a cache. A bear will cover a carcass with sticks and leaves. Sometimes they will drag what they haven't eaten to a different location to tuck it away and disguise the scent. If a cache of meat is large enough, bears have been observed guarding it for five days or longer. In this case, the bear didn't need to make much of a fuss. The coyotes would keep their distance. The men showed no signs of coming back.

The bear pushed brown leaves and a few branches over the blood and the remainder of the food. He walked a few yards away to nestle in by the roots of a tree. He was so tired by that point, after such a feast, that he watched his own eyelids lower. The dark, the quiet, the full belly. He drifted into sleep.

It was a snap that woke him, coming from the edge of the clearing. Something was out there. He lifted his nose, twitched, and was unsurprised to find it was a young bear. They knew each other from the dump and were distantly related, though that didn't really matter to either of them. The larger bear had allowed this younger one to share in his spoils at the dump. Now the young one was hoping for the same to happen again.

It was a foolish wish. Meat at this time of year was scarce. The air was tightening. The sun took a lower course. The first wisps of colder weather had started brushing against them. When a body starts to feel the clenches of cold, it's not a time for sharing.

The large bear made it clear—the young bear should be gone. If he wanted access to the food, he could tangle with the coyotes for the scraps after the larger bear was done.

When the teen didn't leave, the larger bear charged. It was a bluff charge with no contact, a warning. The teen scuttled off, trying to make it look as if he was ashamed, but he wasn't. The teen wanted a few bites and then maybe he would go away. That's what had happened at the dump when he pressed.

The teen crept up again. Here, he found the limit to this interaction. A switch went off inside the larger bear. His next charge wasn't a bluff. The young bear realized what was happening a moment too late. He tried to run, but the large body of the bear came from behind and overwhelmed him. The bite was crushing and hard. A tooth punctured his hide near enough to the neck to scare him. The edge of his ear ripped. He let out such a fearful squeal that it prompted the large bear's jaws to let go.

The lesson was clear. The smaller bear ran off. This time, for good.

The bear went back and stood over the carcass. He lingered long enough to make his intentions clear. If any coyotes or even ravens were watching, the food was still his. He sat down and started to eat again.

Once he was done, he left the remains to the coyotes, smaller bears that might still be lurking, the ravens, the vultures, the flies, the ants, and the worms.

The bear started travelling in a southward direction. As he did, he was inside the northern boundary of Algonquin Park, though he had no way of knowing this. He went east. The month turned. It was September. And then he left the park. There wasn't a fence, but even if there had been, he would never look for something dug in the ground as a marker.

A wilderness park, like Algonquin, is an idea that we have defined by drawing lines on a piece of paper. Like any border, this one is not tangible. It is an imaginary line. It's something we choose to believe in. Luis Alberto Urrea, in *The Devil's Highway*, writes about a border, "maybe it's just an idea nobody can agree on."

The bear's idea of a boundary was a layer of scent. Every animal develops a strategy for processing, organizing, and spreading information. We all specialize depending on our biology and how we live. Humans prize oral and written language. It's the basis for how we collaborate in large groups, but it's a system that excludes other species. What happens when an animal doesn't value stories as much as we do? Fiction is invisible. It doesn't have a smell or leave a trail of pee behind it. You can't eat a story or follow its fragrance in the wind.

The bear left the borders of Algonquin Park. It was fall. It was hunting season.

Part Eight

WHEN TO PLAY DEAD

20.

DURING MY INVESTIGATION, I went to a bar in the hotel where I was staying. The hotel was outside the boundaries of Algonquin Park. I would have preferred to be in a tent in the backcountry, but it was summer. The sun was high during the day. I was struggling with how to stay covered and protect my skin. I decided that an older hotel in a small town, Barry's Bay, on the east side of the park was the next best thing.

The town quadruples its population in the summer. People drive the main street with boats on top of their cars and stock up with food and supplies before heading into Algonquin Park. I liked the bar as it was home to regulars who sat in a line on stools. Eavesdropping on people who know a place is one of my favourite things.

As I was writing up my notes from the interviews I'd done that day, Lady Gaga and Bradley Cooper were singing from a tinny speaker above my head. The walls were studded with wood panelling. A TV showed scrolling headlines: police warning about a rapist targeting women at a university, a car accident, an approaching heat wave.

I ordered a glass of wine. I was in the mood for a celebration. Cancer is a disease of the intangible in the early stages. I couldn't feel the effects of the illness itself, only the operation and the treatment.

I had what felt like invisible borders around me. It took an effort to cross them. Every day became about finding a new way to be. I was using large dollops of sunscreen and wearing clothes with a thicker weave. I liked my wide-brimmed hat. I couldn't limit my UV exposure to zero, but I didn't want to be nocturnal either.

The investigation was taking me farther from home, but more than once I felt trapped and claustrophobic and on the verge of panic, especially in the summer heat. There were no studies of people with my condition to help me set guidelines. I lurched between being too careful and too careless about the sun. It felt as though the giant orb in the sky was out to get me. I didn't know if this was a psychological issue or a reasonable response to what was true. I understood why people often use fighting words when talking about recovery from cancer. A fight, a battle, a war—it's comforting to have a tangible enemy.

But now I was out. In a bar. It felt good to be upright, in a public place, among humans I didn't know, and as close to Algonquin Park as I could get. I started making notes about the day.

I HAD VISITED THE logging museum. At the end of the exhibit, I went into a room set up to explain current logging practices in the park. I stood in front of a panel that explained how trees are harvested. Over 40 percent of Algonquin Park is open to logging. The woman standing beside me let the air out of her lungs in a rush. I turned to look at her, as we had been reading the same section. Her outward expression matched my inward thoughts. "Are you surprised there is still logging in the park?" I asked.

"Yes," she said. "I thought it was protected."

I found the Algonquin Park website on my phone. It doesn't make any attempt to hide logging activity. Just the opposite.

> Algonquin was established in 1893, not to stop logging but to establish a wildlife sanctuary, and by excluding agriculture, to protect the headwaters of the five major rivers, which flow from the park.

The panel and the website stated the facts in a straightforward way, but somehow, after spending so much time in the park, I had managed to hold on to different ideas. I thought of the park as a sanctuary for wildlife and people. Logging didn't fit that image.

Algonquin Park was formed by an Act of Parliament in 1893. The idea behind it came from British colonialists, who applied their ideas about green space to the land in North America. In 1872 the area now known as Yellowstone National Park, in the American West, was created as a "public park or pleasuring-ground for the benefit and enjoyment of the people." In Canada, Algonquin Park was the first provincial park. The name, Algonquin, was suggested to honour "one of the greatest Indian nations that has inhabited the North American continent."

The root word *park* is from the French *parc*, which the *Oxford English Dictionary* cites as appearing in written texts as early as 1260.

It's derived from the idea of an enclosed place set aside by the government and sanctioned by royalty. Parks took on prominence during the reign of Alfred the Great, king of the Anglo-Saxons from 886 to 899. (Many scholars speculate *Beowulf* also came from his court.) Parks were lands used to conserve game for the upper classes to hunt and enjoy. Anglo-Saxon towns had a tradition of another type of space, a village green. This was an enclosed area that was protected, often at the centre of the village, where domestic animals could be kept safe from wolves or wandering people.

But the land in North America wasn't quite like a village green or established hunting grounds for royalty. A wilderness park is a different creature, as Paul Eagles and Grace Bandoh write about Algonquin Park's past. The Germanic word *wilderness* or *wild-deornes* means "land of the wild beast." It mixes in *willed*, meaning "self-willed," and *doer*, an old German word for "animal," and *ness*, a headland—a place where animals make their own rules. In Algonquin Park, these ideas, derived from historical conceptions of parks and wilderness, have been brought together.

Kirby Whiteduck, a chief of the Pikwakanagan First Nation, writes about the impact of Algonquin Park on his people. It may have been officially designated as a park in 1893, but he doesn't see that date as the one with huge significance. His people had filed a petition fifty years before the formation of the park, when the landscape had been completely altered by logging. The petition said, "Our hunting grounds are entirely ruined. Our Beaver and other furs have been destroyed by the constant fires and by the lumbermen in our majestic forests. Our deer have disappeared . . . We are starving."

The park may have been named to honour First Nations people, but when it was created, the First Nations people who lived within its borders were evicted. As the assistant to the commissioner explained at the time, "The presence of the Indians might be a great danger to the preservation of the game in the Park."

I had grown up with the idea that the borders of Algonquin Park were there to protect what lay inside. It was a wild place in a natural state, empty, and waiting to be discovered. Like the oil paintings of the Group of Seven, there is a tradition in Canadian art of rendering pristine landscapes. They are presented and talked about as an ideal version of the wilderness. Similarly, Ansel Adams's grand photos of Yosemite show soaring rock faces and valleys without people or even any trace of them.

"Yours to Discover" is the slogan on Ontario's licence plates.

Robert Jago, a member of the Kwantlen First Nation and Nooksack Indian Tribe, writes about how this idea of wilderness is unrecognizable to him and to many other Indigenous people. To him, the land of places like Algonquin Park never sat empty or untouched. It's always been full of people, animals, and their stories. Every lake and valley had a name.

I SAT IN THE bar, making notes, fighting through a lifetime of confusion. I pulled out my map of Algonquin Park and spread it on the table. I traced the boundaries with a finger. Everything inside was green, a colour I'd always taken to signify nature. To me, Algonquin Park was a haven, a place to recover, untouched and pure. But if I looked at those same borders through another set of eyes, they looked entirely different. Calling Algonquin Park "protected" is accurate only if followed by a question—for whom?

At the top of one of my notebook pages, I had scrawled a line from an essay by William Cronin, written in 1995, about the popular idea of wilderness. He wrote, "Far from being the one place on earth that stands apart from humanity, it is quite profoundly a human creation."

Algonquin Park is a place that people created. It's a cultural idea, and my admiration of nature was more like gazing into a mirror. I started to understand more about why a bear attack shook me to my core: the bear tore through the myths I'd grown up with.

The borders around Algonquin Park had limited my ability to see it clearly before. If a park is set aside as a natural space, what happens when a bear in a wildlife sanctuary, as the official website calls the park, asserts his free will? And what if he kills two people and eats them? The bear was punished by death.

The more I thought about it, the more conflicts kept coming. How can wild animals live in a natural state if we are logging nearly half of their habitat? Is a border protective, does it define a sanctuary, if it's also used to exclude? What if those same lines were used to remove some people? Members of a First Nation, the same one the park was named after, were forced to leave their homes. Their livelihoods were destroyed.

In the bar, I understood that *wilderness-park* isn't a kenning. It's a contradiction.

I had the shaken feeling of a cult member who has finally woken up. A bear attack had forced me to question my faith.

My attention was diverted from the map by friendly banter. Along the bench of the bar were men who seemed to know each other. They chatted comfortably, wore ball caps, and let out wheezy laughs. They sipped brown bottles filled with domestic beer and compared stories about sciatica. One of the older men said carrying a wallet in the back pocket while driving for too many years had sent shooting pains up his right hip.

My glass of wine came. I took a sip. It was dark red and thick enough to chew, and something close to relief threaded through me. It was my first glass in a long time. I hadn't wanted to drink, just as I had trouble caring about eating. My sex drive had barely whispered. My scars had chattered loud enough to take up that space. Now my lungs filled up. My blood seemed to run thicker. My heart pumped and pushed it around.

The wine reminded me of what I'd been missing. There are small pleasures that bring warmth and light to the skin. I let myself feel them. When the larger picture is too overwhelming, it can help to appreciate life on a smaller scale. A glass of wine—it narrowed my scope. It drew my attention exactly to that moment. I lived inside it.

I thanked the waitress and asked her to settle the bill. She pointed toward the bar. "He got it."

I glanced over, and one of the men who sat along the bar pointed his fingers up, a shy hello. He had his arms crossed over the bar, shoulders hunched and head lowered between them. He was the youngest among them, but still of an age to have been, like the rest who sat in the line at the bar, through physio recently. Me too.

I gave him a nod and smiled. I turned back to the waitress and asked her to let him know I wasn't open for business, "but please let him know I appreciate it." She laughed. I stopped to thank him on the way out.

The questions can start small. For me, they began with a glass of wine in a bar. No more.

21.

THE SEARCH PARTY RETURNED to Bates Island a few hours later. Steve Swrjeski had a rifle this time. Other men had them too.

Jerry was in the search party. They handed him a rifle. "What am I going to do with that?" he asked, and handed it right back. He was sent to stand near the western edge of the island to watch in case the bear tried to escape or swim off the back; they wanted him to keep track of where it went. Chris, Jerry's employee, was posted to do the same at the other end of the island.

David Stott walked in a line with the rest of the party to do a search. They found the drag marks, the ones Jerry later showed me with his boot. Something heavy had been pulled through the pine needles. A clear trail started from the area near the fire ring. They followed it up the slope and toward the thick brush near the back of the campsite.

Dave heard someone call out. He looked up the hill and saw the bear. He remembers the bear standing on its hind legs to look at them. His coat was shiny. He looked healthy. There was no mistaking it: a black bear looked down at them.

IT'S SOMETIMES SAID THAT when a bear stands up, he is about to charge. Most experts agree this isn't true. A bear will stand up and look for similar reasons that we do. They want to get a better view and sniff from an upright position.

While Dave was describing the bear, he told me a story I'll never forget. He'd received a call-out one night. There was a report of a human body in the local garbage dump. He was told on the phone that it had no hands or feet and the head was cut off. It was naked and had been left. When Dave arrived, he went to look and confirmed there was a body. It was partly covered with things in the dump, but something struck him as strange. He couldn't quite say what. It wasn't until the coroner came that the answer became completely clear. The body belonged to a black bear. Stripped of his hide and without a head or paws, Dave said the body "looked almost human."

A grizzly bear is in a different weight category. They would be much harder to confuse with a person. Before Bates Island, when I heard stories about bear attacks, I always assumed something had been lost in the telling. An attack on a human didn't fit my image of a black bear; I assumed that the story I'd heard was a case of mistaken identity and that the real perpetrator was a larger grizzly.

Statistically speaking, grizzlies are responsible for more harmful encounters with humans every year than black bears are. Male grizzlies can grow as large as a thousand pounds. The claws on their front paws are around four to six inches long and as sharp as a knife. While these bears aren't necessarily seeking trouble, a human who gets into a tangle with one can be killed with a swipe.

If a grizzly bear had been standing on his hind legs, looking down at the men in the search party, things would have been different. In the event of being attacked by a bear, one of the most repeated pieces of advice is to play dead. This is probably the wrong thing to do if you—like Dave and the men on Bates Island—are facing a predacious black bear.

The play-dead advice applies to grizzly encounters. If you are charged by a grizzly, it is probably a bluff charge. Stand your ground. If you have bear spray, use it to buy yourself some time or space. The US National Park Service (NPS) suggests if a bear is making an aggressive approach, you should start to spray when the bear is about sixty feet away.

If the bear continues to charge, they recommend keeping your pack on if you are wearing one. When I saw a grizzly in the distance in an alpine meadow in Alberta, I took my pack off and backed away from it. I assumed the grizzly would want the chocolate bar in the top pocket as much as I did. But this wasn't smart. A pack will offer some protection for your back and neck, the places a grizzly may focus attention.

Only drop to the ground when and if the grizzly makes contact. In that case, lie on your stomach and clasp your hands around the back of your neck while keeping your elbows at the sides of your face for protection. Stay still. This is playing dead.

The aim with playing dead isn't, as I've heard it explained, that a grizzly won't eat dead things—they aren't that picky. It's to show the bear you aren't a threat. When a human is approached by a grizzly in an aggressive manner, it's likely to be, though not always, a mother with cubs. They have reason to feel threatened. You may have come too close to a food cache.

According to statistics collected by the NPS in Yellowstone since 1970, people who played dead received only minor injuries 75 percent of the time. Those who fought back received severe injuries in 80 percent of encounters. This is a game of odds. You need to weigh them in your favour.

BUT ON THE ISLAND, the men were faced with a black bear that appeared aggressive. Their response needed to be completely different. In this case, don't play dead. A person who puts up less resistance will offer themselves as an easier target.

Dave's mind went back to a bear attack in 1978 near Radiant Lake, northeast of Opeongo Lake. It was mostly reported in the news in the Ottawa area, but I had first heard about it by word of mouth. An eighteen-year-old, Richard, had dropped off three younger boys at Radiant Lake to go fishing. By late afternoon, George, a sixteen-year-old, had caught four speckled trout, which he carried in the pockets of his raincoat. He decided to fish some more and went up a creek by himself. Mark and Billy, the two younger boys, decided to follow him along the creek sometime later.

Richard had dozed off in the car. When he woke, he drove up and down the dirt road looking for the boys. He called out. He blew the horn.

On the eastern side of the park, where they were, the elevation is slightly lower. It is boggy in places. The bush is dense. Where the lake narrows into the mouths of rivers, the brush seems to cling tight to the ground. The water rushes quickly and it can be hard to hear your companions. You can think someone is right behind you, then turn to see the landscape empty. The footing can be wet, sticky, and uneven. Downed branches spread out to whip your shins and catch your toes. The mud gives your boots a good suck. The trees start to look the same and the foliage thickens. A body can easily get spun around.

When Richard couldn't find the boys, he left to call for help. The police were called by midnight. Two hundred searchers came out. There were helicopters and tracking dogs. Soon, there were three hundred searchers, and by the time the bodies were found, nearly four hundred people were involved.

It was a bear who led the searchers to the bodies. They saw a large male hovering over a specific area only about five hundred feet from where the car had been parked, the same place the boys were supposed to meet. As the father of one of the boys later said in an interview, "There were twenty of us there and still the bear wouldn't move." The bear refused to let the searchers get close to the area he was guarding. They decided to shoot him.

A conservation officer, Lorne O'Brien, came in. He described how the bear walked away from the area but then circled back around. O'Brien shot the bear from about a hundred yards away. "He didn't appear to be anything but normal to me. He was looking at me, but he wasn't aggressive." O'Brien filed a departmental report that gave more detail. "I shot it. He went down with the first shot; it was hit through the shoulders. He kept trying to get up and I shot him again firing a few times. It was difficult to see as it was getting dark."

The bodies of the boys were found in a bear cache, partially buried with dirt and leaves, and within ten feet of each other. Two of the bodies were harder to see, almost completely hidden.

The boys were young and respected, and they had spent time in the outdoors. No one thought they had done anything to bring the attack on, but some people wondered if they had made a mistake with their catch. George's raincoat still had the fish in the pockets, not a great place to keep them. There were signs that he had struggled to get the coat off. It was found away from the bodies, snagged on a branch in the creek. Had the scent of fish drawn the bear to the boys?

It doesn't stand up to scrutiny. Thousands of people go fishing in Algonquin Park every year. Millions do the same across North America. They handle fish, put them in coolers, buckets, maybe even pockets, but none of this brings on a bear attack.

Also, the bear didn't eat the fish after the attack. They were still in the pocket of the jacket, untouched.

The bear's head was removed and flown to Ottawa for tests. No sign of disease was found. (Rabies has yet to be found as the likely cause of any attack.) The testing did reveal slight abnormalities in the brain from an old parasitic infection, but this was at a level thought to be fairly typical. There was no sign of encephalitis, a viral infection, and no brain tumour. Tests for mercury poisoning proved negative.

What kind of bear would do this? Hank Rietveld, the fish and wildlife supervisor in the park, said he "had no idea why the bear would attack." The father of one of the boys, who had decades of experience in the wilderness, couldn't square this behaviour with what he knew of bears. He thought the bear must have snuck up on the boys, that they couldn't hear it because of the rushing water. He told a reporter it was "improbable that a male would attack."

In 1978, it was thought that a mother with cubs was more likely to show aggressive behaviour. Some people had happened across cubs, whether by accident or for other reasons. The mother would woof, snort, paw the ground, and maybe charge. She might swipe or bite if feeling particularly threatened. An official told a reporter that a female must have been separated from her cubs, then "went berserk and attacked." This was perceived wisdom at the time. "A female, when she feels her cubs are in danger, is dynamite," a man said to a journalist.

It was in this context that Dr. Stephen Herrero started collecting data about black bear attacks. He found patterns that contradicted the perceived wisdom. It wasn't a mother and her cubs that presented the risk. Herrero established that, when it came to black bear attacks, it was usually the large, older males who approached humans as prey.

BACK ON BATES ISLAND, this fit the description of the bear the men found. When the bear saw the search party, he could have turned around and, in a flash, moved up the last stretch to the height of land. Within seconds, he would have been up and over the crest. Once he was on the other side, the men wouldn't have had a clear line of sight. On the other hand, if the bear ran down the slope, jumped into the water, and swam away, there was still a chance he would be caught.

Jerry and Chris were positioned to keep watch. Two boats were in the water doing the same, but there would have been some initial confusion if the bear had chosen to try to escape by water. Everyone involved would have been uncertain enough to hesitate. The search would have had to change from a defensive stance to an offensive chase, not easy considering the circumstances. During that moment, the bear might have slipped away.

Instead, the bear charged.

Over short distances, black bears have been clocked at speeds of thirty miles an hour or more. Like a bolt, he came crashing through the brush. Dave found it hard to describe the speed. He pushed a hand forward. "It happened fast."

This was no bluff. The bear was serious about trying to run the search party off the island. Not only were they intruding on his space, they were doing something much worse: they were moving toward his cache of meat.

As the bear charged the men, logic, reasoning, and rational explanations were cast aside. There was no time for a planned reaction. Instinct took over. Fear is a primary sensation. Nerves are sharp, eyes wide; terror moves through the body like electricity.

Philosopher Wayne Davis makes a meaningful distinction about fear. There is a first kind of fear, an emotional state that involves involuntary arousal, a fast heartbeat, sweat, and trembling. This is different from the second kind, the fear we feel when we think that something could, or might, happen. The second response is an attitude that can be altered, rather than an instinctive response. A person might be able to learn to have more control over it.

There is no doubt that the men felt only the first kind of fear in that moment. Their bodies kicked into a range of reactions, to run, fight, or freeze.

Swrjeski put his rifle's telescopic sight to his eye. Another person, an individual with less training or different wiring, might have struggled with nerves, blurred vision, or shaking fingers under this pressure. Fear isn't always a compatible emotion to manage while aiming for precision. Bears have thick hides. There are many accounts of people only injuring a bear with a bullet, making it mad and provoking an attack.

But Swrjeski was a practised shot. He had trained as an officer and in the field as a hunter. He wounded the bear with the first shot, which stopped the charge. He killed the bear in two.

22.

IT WAS MID-SEPTEMBER, ONE month before the attack. The bear was outside the park's boundaries to the north and east. This was part of his range, the elliptical orbit that he travelled every year. It was boggy and mucky where he was walking, the lower side of the park. He found a small dirt road he had traversed a few years back. It made travelling easier, a nice smooth surface, and not as many branches to crash through. Bears and people sometimes meet because they both like to take the easy route.

The road the bear was on led to a few houses. The bear sniffed the garbage cans of one, but they were empty. The house was a cottage, and the owners had gone south for the winter. Another house had a bird feeder with seed inside. He gave it a swat and it swung wildly on the hinges for a moment until it came crashing down. From there it only took one more smash for all the seeds to come spilling out. He cracked them between his teeth.

A bird feeder might not seem like an obvious target for a bear, but Jeremy Inglis points out that one feeder can contain twenty thousand calories in one easy container. It would take a full day of feeding on blueberries to get the same energy. The many videos of bears getting into bird feeders are proof that they will attract bears. If you live in bear country, it's better to find other ways of admiring the birds.

The bear kept following the road until it became more like a path. It was an unofficial access route that would eventually lead to Algonquin Park. Sometimes it was used by cross-country skiers in the winter, occasionally by hikers, but this time of year it was mostly hunters.

A pickup truck was parked as far up the road as it could drive and not get stuck. The bear ambled by.

In the distance, coming toward the bear, was a group of three hunters. They wore boots and bright jackets to stand out against the foliage. They had .30-calibre rifles slung across their shoulders. They were walking out of the park after an unproductive day. They were discussing whether they should go to one of the lodges that baited the bears to draw them in. You could go out with a guide and be guaranteed a kill.

After a while, one of the men started to question their direction. Shouldn't they be at the truck by now? Had they overshot? Another knew they only had to follow the old road. Even though it was washed out and grown over, it was clear they were on it.

"Just a few more minutes," he said.

"A few?"

"Like twenty."

They were tired and hungry, the last of their water drunk a few hours back. It would be nice to get home, have a few beers, and order pizza. They put their heads down and focused on putting one foot in front of the other. They walked in silence, slightly miserable now, getting cold. One of them had a blister on his heel.

For the first half of the twentieth century, black bears were considered vermin, pests, or nuisance animals like rats or raccoons. In Ontario in 1961, they were classified as managed game. A licence is needed to hunt them.

In the years after the Bates Island attack, from 1992 to 1994, when Jeremy Inglis and Mike Wilton studied twenty-five male bears, they recorded that six of them had died. Two were identified as problem bears and shot. Outside the boundaries of Algonquin Park, hunters shot the other four.

The bush was thick and twisted where the old road wound. The bear walked slowly along the opening, taking his time. When he hit a slope, he would cut toward a stream he liked. The seeds from the bird feeder raid were good, but they'd made him thirsty. He liked to stick his tongue out in a pool and let the water rush around it. Sometimes he stuck his nose in and blew out. The bubbles would burst up and tickle as they broke. He was thinking about that sensation when he heard a gasp.

The bear looked up to see three men about sixty yards away. The four of them all stood frozen in surprise. In their minds, the three men had already ended their day—not one of them had imagined bumping into a bear by mistake. It was something they couldn't do when they were trying. One of them started to move.

The bear let out a woof as a warning. He could charge to scare them, but he knew a gun. He'd never been hit, but the sound when a gun was fired drove him crazy. It was enough to turn any creature with good ears right off them. Too loud, it felt like a crack to the skull. And the residue, that fine, powdery burn.

The mental calculation came as fast as a glance. There were three men. One of him. Around him, the land was thick with trees. He could duck and weave and lose them with no problem. There was no pride lost in running or to be gained in fighting. With one of his own kind, there was often food or mating at stake. His social standing and reputation were important. In this case, though, it was nothing. He didn't want anything to do with these men.

IN CANADA, AROUND TWENTY thousand black bears are legally hunted every year. It's about twice that number in the United States. The true number is higher when poaching is taken into account, and even higher when kills in the defence of property are tallied—if a bear breaks into a cottage, for example. There is a debate about the need for hunting black bears to control numbers, but there is no question about which species is the more aggressive. Since the turn of the last century, the number of humans killed by a black bear on average every year: one.

IN THE TIME IT took one of the men to blink, the bear turned and bolted. The brush crashed around him.

With the bear now on the move, everything changed. Two of the men barely saw him, a blur of black in the distance. But for the third man, things slowed down. His rifle was already in his hands. He lifted the sight to his eye and squeezed.

The gun fired. He watched through the sight, a blur of black fur and green leaves and branches swinging. He held the rifle steady, but there wasn't another shot to take. The bear was gone. It was hard to see anything: the light was flat, and the dark spaces between the trees would soon swallow them.

"Holy shit," the guy in the back said, still catching up. "What was that?"

"A bear." The man lowered his gun. "Huge. Like three hundred pounds."

"No way."

"Did you hit it?" asked his other friend.

They waited for a moment. They all knew the danger of not getting a clear shot. Hitting a bear with a bullet but not killing him was a good way to make him angry. They had all heard stories about an injured bear charging in a fury. Was he that big, really? None of them had got a good look at him.

THERE'S A TENDENCY AMONG all outdoors people to overestimate the size of a bear. Like reports of a fish, the guesses tend to be on the high side. When I was reading about the Radiant Lake attack, the first estimate I found in the newspaper articles was that the bear weighed about 400 pounds. With a bit of distance, the figure started to lower. A few days later the number was revised to more than 300 pounds, then it slid down to a more realistic 275.

THE MEN WAITED. A crashing in the distance, then nothing. The bear was gone. They looked at each other, one shrugged uneasily, then they started back to the truck.

Bears' ears are sensitive. They can be swivelled in any direction to pick up sounds. Like a dog, bears catch a greater range of frequencies, especially at the high end of the register. The mechanical noise of the gun, before it fired, came to the bear in distinct steps. Each served as a warning—the *chunk* of the latch, the rasping metal, the ring of the shell slipping backwards.

By the time the gun had fired, the bear was already running at full speed. His explosive muscles fired alongside the gas expanding from the muzzle of the rifle. The bullet split from the barrel as his haunches curled. His claws dug into the soft earth, the large paws spread and pressed, and his limbs stretched to propel him across the land.

The sound of the gun firing came like a physical blow. The pressure found the bear first. It rushed against the pad of his nose and struck the bone of his skull. It punched through the longer guard hairs of his ears, parted the soft fuzz inside, and burst painfully against the drums.

The bullet didn't hit the bear. It ripped past his body, missing by a few feet to the right side. The tip bit into a tree and pierced the bark skin. The bullet lodged deep into the meat of the trunk, splitting the wood, until it stopped near the core.

Long after a human would think it was gone, the sound of the gun continued to cling to the bear. The pale-white smell turned grey, but the echo didn't leave him. It lingered inside his ears as a memory he could feel, the sensitive hairs held it, and the delicate mechanics of the small bones of his inner ear continued to shudder.

Finally, when he started to slow, the air still buzzed. The bear had a quiver in his lip. A pain became associated with the men, a shard of anger, a rumbling fury. His irritation was far greater than when a younger bear got a tooth into him. It was about the bear's place on the land.

Especially in recent years, the bear had been the one who held his ground. The concession he'd made to the men wasn't a tangible loss, but it left a bruise. It lodged deep inside his muscles like a reminder.

In the distance, the choke of an engine. Nose to the wind, the bear put the men behind him. He found the ridge, farther down the drainage than he'd intended to be, but there was a place with a nice pool. He drank, sticking his tongue in the cool water, allowing the rush to flow around it.

Soon, he found a sheltered spot to curl up by a tree. Once settled, he licked the back of his paw and rubbed his ears to soothe them.

Part Nine

HOW TO BE BRAVE

23.

ONCE I HAD INTERVIEWED every person on my list, I drove back to Toronto. I had uncovered as many facts as I could about what happened on Bates Island that evening. A couple took a small motorboat to an island. A black bear attacked them. He killed them. A broken oar was found on the campsite. It was a rare predacious attack. It was a tragedy. There was nothing I could do to make it better. I had uncovered the information that was out there. It felt as though I'd come to the end of what there was to learn.

Had I tamed my brain with facts? No, I'd run out of questions to ask.

I hit a low point that summer. I would get the urge to curl into a ball and sleep. Nothing but a two-hour nap would fix it. On some days I could barely keep my head up. When I tried to describe the sensation to Dave, it sounded too subjective. I couldn't decide if I was speaking about how I felt or talking about a larger problem. What was my true condition? Was I overreacting? Or was I being complacent and allowing cancer to spread all through me?

I was barely making it through daily life. It was eight months since the surgery, long enough that I thought I should have regained my strength. My faulty CDKN2A gene means I'm at an increased risk for secondary cancers. Pancreatic is the most common, but cancer in the brain, cervix, and throat are statistical possibilities. New research is finding more connections.

I decided to treat my condition as Stephen Herrero might approach it. I started taking notes and tracking my symptoms by time and date. This was a way to build objectivity and evidence around my personal experience. When you feel this way, is it a problem in your mind or body? The problem lies in the assumptions behind that question. There isn't a way to separate the two.

I took my notebook of data to my family doctor.

Dr. Toubassi had seen me in many different states. With cancer more recently, but also through the births of two babies, breastfeeding, immunizations, colds, coughs, fevers, and everything else parenthood manages to throw at you. I saw a look of concern on her face. She suspected there was something fundamental going on. We briefly discussed the possibilities of other cancer and methods for screening. She thought for a moment and made a motion with her hand as if to stay, "Stop."

She explained, partly for the benefit of the resident doctor who was with us, that in medical school she was taught a process for solving problems. What she described was much like what Dave Stott had described. Don't get caught up in drama or engage with the emotion. Collect evidence and follow the trail to a diagnosis.

"Let's see if there is something simple first," she said. "We'll go from there."

A few hours later, I sat at my computer with a blank document open. The white page was the perfect reflection of my mind. I didn't have the energy to write, not truth or fiction. The phone rang. It was Dr. Toubassi.

Seeing her name on my phone startled me. For the previous ten months, her phone calls had brought bad news. Her name on the screen of my phone made my heart thump. When I picked up, though, her voice sounded different. It came with a lift. "I got your test results," she said. "It's great news. You need to eat a steak!"

My iron levels were way down.

It is one of the most common nutritional deficiencies in North America. Iron is a necessary component for the body to make hemoglobin, the protein in red blood cells that allows them to carry oxygen. My body was starved for it. This explained so much, about why I was so tired, dragging my feet, short of breath, and often weepy (I cringe when I think of the bear experts who have seen me cry). I felt dumb for missing such a basic thing. I had lost many of my primal urges, including my appetite.

This was news about my health that had a concrete solution.

For every species, biology shapes their reality. Mammals, bears and humans, need certain things to live and thrive, and these are more than cravings. That my blood needs minerals to make oxygen isn't up for debate. Neither is my mutation. The only way to go forward and thrive, as a human, is to observe these basic biological facts.

I started eating steak and spinach and chicken and eggs. I took supplements, and a few weeks later I was no longer having nap attacks. Soon, the breath came back into my lungs. I could hold my head up. I still took naps, but only because I love them. Slowly, I started being able to walk easily and build muscle.

I sat in our kitchen. Dave had gone to the butcher and cooked a glistening slab of steak. I cut into it, the meat sliced easily, and a shiver tingled down my spine. I was reminded of a thing we often push to the back of our minds, that we are made of something similar. One animal eats another. The steak was medium-rare. The blood ran out as gravy. There was marbled fat along the edge. I cut the slice in two and took a bite. I closed my eyes as I chewed.

WHILE MY HEALTH AND mind improved, cancer continued to make moves. I found a black spot in my eye. It looked like a freckle on the white part between my iris and the bridge of my nose. I couldn't see it when looking straight on, but I could when I glanced to the side. It had a creeping feeling about it.

The specialist, an eye surgeon, agreed it might be trouble. He said I had two choices. I could assume it was melanoma and do eye chemotherapy, three months of eye drops. When he explained how irritated my eye would be, he said, "You will hate me." The second option was to remove the lesion and see if it was cancer. They could do the procedure in the office. I'd be able to go home after. We could decide treatment after a diagnosis.

I couldn't imagine opting to do chemo. I didn't even have to think about it. Surgery was for me. It was scheduled within the week.

When I arrived at the office, I was still wondering why anyone in my position would opt for chemo. I asked myself that question right until the moment I lay back in the chair. The surgeon and the nurse were busy disinfecting. I was in what felt like a dentist's chair and glanced at the metal tray beside me. There lay a scalpel.

If you have seen the film *A Clockwork Orange*, I don't need to describe the kind of clamp they used to pry my eyelid open. The surgeon put numbing drops into my eye.

I didn't feel anything after that, but watched the surgeon draw on my eye white to mark the spot. I could read the brand name that was printed on the plastic case of the pen. Because of the position of the freckle, I had to be awake to look up and to the side so that my eye was in the correct position. I was told to hold still. There was no need to ask about the consequences of moving. Luckily, I didn't cough or sneeze. I never asked why I wasn't tied down, but I guess my compliance had to be voluntary.

The steel blade moved directly into my line of vision. I couldn't look away, hide my eyes, or even blink. I had to watch.

A white Q-tip moved into my line of vision. It dabbed. It pulled away dripping red. This continued. There was a blast of freezing. I watched a needle duck and bob to pull the two stitches through. The surgeon was skilful, precise, and what he was able to do was almost mesmerizing. It was also horrifying.

Once done, I walked into the reception area to find Dave waiting. When he asked how it went, I struggled to put words to it. "A horror movie filmed in first person?"

I had a white patch over one eye. I didn't look as much like a pirate as I would have liked, or if I resembled one, it was because I appeared to be drunk. My depth perception was off. I managed to sway my way to the elevator and, in an act of overcompensation, designated myself as the button pusher. I asked the woman beside me what floor she wanted. I jabbed and missed the panel of buttons altogether.

We walked along College Street to get home. It's a twenty-minute walk, I wasn't in pain, and I thought walking would help my one eye adjust. I did hear Dave sigh when I suggested it, but he grabbed my arm and we started off.

When two people spend a lot of time together, they can start to function like an organism. It's called physiological linkage. For example, the heart rate of one person can influence the pulse of the other, or hormone levels will influence those of a lover, and a bout of nerves can be passed on. When I lie on Dave's chest, my breathing slows down to sync with his. I feel calmer when he is close. The warmth of his body is relaxing. Dave was my balance. Now he became my eyes. I needed him as I never had before. It is scary to need someone so completely. At the same time, I was aware that life is short. If an end is certain, every moment we have becomes more important.

The vision in my good eye had narrowed into a tunnel. I've walked that way many times, but didn't recognize my surroundings. Things came in flashes, red lights blinking, a foot dodging, a puff of warm air from a vent, the smell of pee at the corner with a square of cement, the sound of the streetcar breaking on metal rails, a high, grinding squeal, and a flash of its red body going by. Walking down College Street felt like a great wilderness adventure.

THE BOYS PLAYED MINI-HOOP in our main-floor room. They were banging the small ball into a small net over and over.

We installed the net as a survival tactic during the pandemic. The dining room has served as centre court many times since. Between shots, we were having a conversation about one of Max's classmates. It was the kind of talk that comes most easily with teenagers when there is no danger of eye contact. Ben took a shot while I asked if Max's friend was okay. The friend's father had died in difficult circumstances recently.

I told the boys I was asking because my dad had died when I was young too. "And you guys know some of the feeling too, because I've been sick."

"But you didn't actually have cancer," said Max. His tone was matter-of-fact.

I paused, confused by the statement. He had seen the stitches along my back. Many times, he had climbed up two flights of stairs to lie in bed and keep me company.

"They were just checking to see if it was cancer, right?" He stopped, knees bent, ball in hand, just short of taking a shot, and looked me in the eyes, waiting for my answer.

As a mother with teens, my daily refrain was "You weren't listening." My first reaction was to say it again, but something stopped me.

Before my surgery, we sat down with the boys. I told them what was going to happen. I'd be laid up for a while. They knew that part, but Max looked at me in such a plain way, I realized we had only spoken about the first step. I told them that the doctors were checking to see if the cancer had spread. Maybe I delivered the good news that the doctors hadn't found any signs that it had, but I'd spoken in clipped terms, indirectly, and used a verbal workaround. Underneath Max's question, I could see that, from his perspective, I'd sidestepped the difficult part of the conversation.

I thought of my dad. He was weak and on the edge of death. His body had been wasted by a disease and a brutal regimen of chemotherapy, but he still summoned the courage to talk to me.

Where did his courage come from? Knowing his obsessions, he might have thought of the hero, Beowulf, as an older king. After fifty years of ruling over a peaceful land, the third monster arrived, a dragon. "A flame-tongued one who sought out strongholds as she scourged, a slip-skinned dragon, tagging the sky with flaming sigils." She was the most terrifying of the three monsters Beowulf faced. As dark as the clouds, with breath as hot as the sun, she burned their houses and crops. She was a storm that threatened their existence.

J.R.R. Tolkien, an Old English scholar who taught my dad, and also a renowned author, suggested that the dragon represents the evening of the hero's life. Beowulf was older and in weak condition when he faced the battle with the dragon. "This'll be the battle that breaks your king," Beowulf said to his men.

My dad may have thought of that line in the poem. Beowulf knew what was going to happen and turned to face it. A hero is a person who makes a brave decision. The size of a heroic feat is directly related to the circumstances the hero finds herself in.

When my dad told me he was dying, he had already lost the battle. The fatal wound was inflicted. He knew what was happening as he turned to look into the vulnerable face of his child and said the hardest thing.

There was a difference between when my dad died and my present circumstances. My cancer hadn't spread. Even if my risk was high, I wasn't dying. Not yet. I had caught my cancer much earlier. And when my dad died, the human genome hadn't been mapped. We didn't know as much about a genetic legacy and how cancer is passed on. I could be screened. Finding the cancer early is the best way to improve my lifespan. And every year the treatments are progressing. In the past five years, the statistics for surviving cancer have grown much more favourable.

But as I looked at my son, standing by the net, I realized why I had avoided the conversation. For the first time, I confronted my true fear.

Cancer attacks in silence. In slow motion. There wouldn't be a snapping twig, a musky smell, or a dark shape in the woods. I'd have no warning. The approach would come by way of an ultrasound, a blood test, or an MRI. I would find out it had spread in a clinical setting, dressed in a blue robe that didn't tie properly. I'll never be able to grab an oar and split it across cancer's back. There is no way to stick a shining sword into the belly of the dragon and slay a disease that comes from my own cells.

I knew I was brave. I could suffer, be cut, go through rounds of medication, and none of that mattered. I was tough and could weather hard things. What I couldn't face was the 50 percent chance that I had passed the mutation on to my sons.

All I wanted was to pick up my sword and go to battle and fight that bear. Right there, in that moment, sitting in a chair, watching a game of mini-hoop, I wanted to fight for their lives. With all my strength, I would roar, lunge, and leap. And if I was fatally wounded, if I died shortly after the battle, that was okay. I could die for love. I could die knowing that I'd defended them to the end. But it wasn't how the battle would go.

I would die for my kids, but I couldn't fight cancer for them.

The battleground, one I had been anticipating for years, wasn't going to be on a campsite in the deepest wilderness. It was in my house. And the moment of truth wasn't going to be dramatic either. It would be ordinary. Like any other day, it would appear with the afternoon light coming through the front window, a puff of dog hair by the chair leg, and a smudge of fingerprints running alongside the stairs.

Instead of raising a sword, I had to find the strength. I had to walk directly toward the things that might hurt, no matter how terrifying I found it. I had to respect my kids enough to know that, in the face of a battle, they could find courage too.

"Yes," I said with a deep breath. "I have cancer. The same kind as my dad."

Max stopped, ball in hand. "Are you going to die?" He paused before taking his shot.

"Probably." I smiled.

"Everyone dies," said Ben, answering the call of being a protective big brother.

"Soon?" Max asked.

"Not yet," I said. "The cancer hasn't spread. We caught it quickly."

"When?"

"I don't know."

Max shrugged, then took the shot at the mini-hoop. He missed and quickly became caught up in fighting his brother for control of the ball. A young mind lives in the moment, easily concerned and easily distracted. Game on.

I watched them play and knew I'd done it. I'd moved toward

the thing that scared me the most. It was fine. And something strange happened that I hadn't expected. I felt braver for it. I've long believed that love doesn't work as a zero-sum equation. The more love you give, the more love there is to go around. I started to realize that being brave might be the same.

I'd been so caught up in dying that I'd forgotten something more important. I needed to focus on being alive.

In the face of death, it felt scary to want to live. It was a risk. My chances weren't great. It might not work out, but life is all or nothing. I needed to be brave enough to turn and start moving in that direction. Love was the only thing strong enough to pull me.

24.

STEVE SWRJESKI'S FIRST BULLET had stopped the bear's charge. It lodged near his chest. When the second bullet hit his head, he dropped and didn't move again. Soon, the bear was pronounced dead.

It was understood then, and still is, that a bear who has successfully preyed on a human might try it again. This leaves officials in a difficult position. They had to kill the bear.

The police allowed everyone on the island to break formation. There was some banter among the men. Some of them started teasing Swrjeski for missing the first shot. It was the kind of gallows humour that acts as an acknowledgement; Swrjeski had likely saved a life or two.

One of the men climbed to where the bear had been standing. That was when they found the bodies.

The temperature that day reached a high of around nine degrees Celsius. It wasn't raining, but all the men described the island as having a grim feeling. Before their eyes, it had changed from a beautiful place into a crime scene. Rather than seeing the vibrant leaves, the dappled sun through the branches, or the shimmer of the lake, their eyes would pick up cues that matched what they imagined might have happened. Even if they didn't know the whole story, they would focus on certain details that held clues—the knocked-over chair, the split oar, and the dark shadows between the trees.

Jerry went up to the bodies to look at them. As the son of a butcher, he understood that, as much as we all try to resist the idea, we are all made of the same things underneath. "I was so curious."

He also went to look at the bear. He showed me the spot where he walked up to it, on the slope well above the campsite, but not yet at the height of land. The shrubs and the brush had grown up in the meantime, but it was much the same as he remembered it in 1991. It is far enough back that it doesn't get the same kind of foot traffic as the flattened part of the campsite down lower to the water.

Jerry touched the bear. "This thing is still warm," he remembers thinking.

He remembers kneeling over the bear's body. He had never been that close to one before. We are sensitive to life. The process of death isn't talked about much, but many people say they can tell when something is dead. That said, we often delegate an official verdict to a scientific test, a pulse, a heartbeat monitor, the squiggly line of a brain wave.

Buddhism defines life in two ways. The first is the simple act of possessing heat, the ability of a body to convert the energy with a metabolism. The second is sentience, meaning an organism can sense, experience, and take action. Whether Buddhist or not, we are good at picking up these cues. Many of us feel them on an intuitive level. And Jerry had that sense from the bear—this was a life that had only just passed by. There was still something vital in it.

"Have you seen the size of a bear's canines?" Jerry showed me how he pulled back the bear's lips. He described the teeth. "I had my fingers up in the gums, looking at the canines, going—are you fucking kidding?" He remembered they were about two and a half inches long and as big around as a finger. They weren't sharp, but massive.

Jerry poked the bear's ears and claws. He pulled the skin back on the paws to look closely. "Again, you're going—holy shit." These were like weapons, daggers, or talons. Our bodies don't have anything like it. He touched the fur. I asked him if it was thick and glossy, like I'd seen in a photo. "Exactly," he said.

Jerry had a solo canoe trip planned for the days after the attack. He knew it wasn't rational to think he would be attacked, but that didn't mean he wasn't terrified. "The fear, that's what bothered me about it. It was totally out of my control." He decided to go anyway.

On that trip, he sat up for most of the night, his back to the water, and built up the fire. He stared into the dark woods, watching, listening for the snap of a twig, and expecting to see something coming. "It didn't feel voluntary. I couldn't stop it."

In the years after, Jerry learned much more about black bears, which is what helped him cope. He learned how to read their behaviour. Since, he has encountered bears a handful of times. They coexist just fine. He has never experienced any aggression.

I have respect for Jerry's approach. He went right up to the bear and looked at it closely. After touching the bear, feeling the fur, ears, and teeth, there was no mistaking what this could be. He knew this wasn't a monster or some kind of demon. Later, he could demystify it. He felt the body, still warm, the heart only just stopped beating, its life gone. It was a way to return a body, a myth, to what it was. Not a monster, a rogue, or a demon, but a bear.

The men on the island started documenting evidence. They found signs that an altercation had taken place between a bear and a human near the beach at the front of the campsite. There was no sign of a human moving around after the struggle. In the dirt and thick layer of pine needles, time is tracked by layers. The most recent events take place at the top.

The things that appeared on the surface, the most recent layer, were drag marks. They were wide, made by a body, the marks Jerry later described to me by moving the toe of his boot through the pine needles. They went up toward the ridge.

The remains of the bodies were found more than three hundred yards up from the shoreline of the campsite, in four or five piles. They found Ray's body first. His shirt and trousers were stripped back in a similar way to what a bear will do with an animal hide. He had a belt around his waist. His calves were partially eaten.

Not long after, they found Carola. She was mostly gone. The recovered remains only weighed about thirty pounds. The muscle had been stripped from her arm, from fingers to shoulder. The bones were picked clean, but not broken. Her watch remained on her wrist, with the flesh underneath still intact.

Both bodies had been partially covered with leaves and debris. A cache.

The distance from the firepit to the cache area is an easy walk, but if I were dragging something half my size or larger, it would take some effort. The ground is packed hard, but as evidenced by the marks through the pine needles left behind, the dirt gives some resistance. The slant isn't steep, but it is a sufficient incline to make gravity work against you.

A government biologist named George Kolenosky went to the island a few weeks after the attack. He found sleeping areas, not dens for hibernating but indications of a bear curling up for the night. He also found trails and signs that indicated the bear had been hanging around for some time.

The bear wasn't attracted to the island by humans or food. When the couple arrived, he was already on the island.

25.

TWO WEEKS BEFORE THE attack, at the turn of October, the bear wandered on familiar terrain. After the summer crowds of people in the park had diminished, he moved closer to the park's heart. He was east of Opeongo Lake now. He travelled down the length of the lake from the north, sometimes taking the service road, sometimes walking across warm flanks of rock or through open meadows. In the middle of the day, he sat at the edge of a marsh with his belly in the mud to cool down. The cattails swayed.

In late summer and autumn, bears enter a stage of eating and drinking called hyperphagia. They fatten up in anticipation of the coming long winter nap. Studies have found that black bears who have access to unlimited food eat as much as 15,000 to 20,000 calories per day during hyperphagia. It's a binge. One theory is that the amount of sunlight in the day, and its angle, triggers a bear to eat to excess and get ready for hibernation. I know people who report similar impulses with the coming of a Canadian winter.

One morning the bear slipped into the water at the edge of Opeongo Lake. Bears will wade, soak, and dip into water to cool down. He had a memory of the white suckers that spawned in the creek in the spring. There were still a few berries clinging to the bushes. The breeze was gentle. The air was cooler.

He worked his way toward a grove of beech trees on the mainland to the southeast of Bates Island. Beech trees are hardwood with a smoother, silvery-grey bark. They grow large and spread like a maple. The stand that the bear preferred had trees that were closer together. The leaves were still green and fluttering.

He climbed up one of the tallest trees to a spot where three branches grew out from each other. In the middle was a kind of cradle, the perfect place for a bear to sit. He started to break branches around where he sat in a cluster. Each branch he chose was studded with prickly nuts. He stretched out to collect as many of these twigs and branches as he could and pulled them to his comfortable spot.

He started to eat. The beech nuts are held in a spiky pod. When ripe, they pop open. Inside, the nuts are a gold mine of nutrition for bears or humans. Each nut is full of fats and proteins. He would strip the nuts off the branch, pop them in his mouth, spit out the shells, and chew. He did this over and over, until a pile of branches collected around him.

Once the bear had plucked all the nuts he could reach from the first tree, he climbed another and started eating more. He dozed, rested, woke up, yawned, and ate. A few other bears came by. A mother with cubs moved close. Her babies had been born in the spring. They had grown, but were still too small to defend themselves. The large bear could be a danger. The mother had her cubs scamper up a tree while she took the measure of the situation.

A tree is the preferred escape route for cubs around Algonquin Park. Whenever I've watched a mother bear send her cubs to safety, it looks like a human mother telling her kids to scoot. In a tree, the cubs are safer from larger black bears, wolves, grizzlies if they are in the area, and humans. The cubs wait until they get a sign that it's safe to come down.

Jeremy Inglis told me a story that illustrates the potential perils. He was tracking a black bear they had tagged. The bear stopped to spend time near White Partridge Lake, which is northeast of Opeongo. Jeremy wanted to know what the bear was doing and went on foot to see what he could find. He found an ash tree with a broken branch at the top. Down the trunk were claw marks that took the shape of a spiral and dragged, as if a bear had been hanging on. Inglis followed the marks down and found the remains of a female bear. She had been chased into a tree, grabbed by the leg, and dragged down. She was killed and eaten. The bear had moved on, but Jeremy found bear scat, or poop, with bear hair inside it. A bear had pursued the female, taken a chance, dragged her out of the tree, and eaten her.

THE MOTHER BEAR STAYED at the edges of the stand of trees and watched until the male gave her a signal that he wasn't feeling threatened or aggressive. There were plenty of nuts. More than any one bear, or five, could eat. He didn't mind having them around. Like at the dump, when food was ample, the company was welcome.

She gathered her cubs and they all went up a tree together. She showed them how to harvest the nuts, and soon they were content and full in their nest of branches. It became a place the cubs would return to again and again.

When the male bear was finished feeding, he climbed down from the beech tree and lifted his snout toward the gentle breeze coming from the direction of the island. He stood near the edge of the water. He knew the island often had people on it during the busier summer. But the island was empty, and so he went.

He plunged his large body into the channel. He waded on the sand, the soft bottom allowing each paw to sink a few inches. After the rain, it was deep enough to swim that year. When the current picked up, he started an easy paddle. He was agile and buoyant in the water. He kept his nose up and let out a series of small snorts as he swam. From a distance, he sounded like a person blowing through a snorkel, but he wasn't trying to be quiet. There was no one around. There was no need for caution.

Pull a human from the water and the first thing they will do is wipe their eyes to be able to see. For the bear, when water dripped inside his long snout, everything around him became less clear. For that reason, when he swam, he held his snout at a slight angle and blew out. He didn't want water to get in.

He swam toward the closest point of land, feet touching down again on the sandbar between the mainland and the island. By that time of year, his fur was full and thick. The oils inside it were heavy and held the water away from the innermost layers of skin. His undercoat was ready for the winter and the cold didn't bother him. If you put a hand on it, you would have to work your fingers in to get them down far enough to touch the skin. The fat along his rump and back kept him warm.

There was a bite on his haunches; the bump marked where a tick had burrowed. Earlier in the day he had stood on his hind legs and rubbed it raw against the bark of a tree. The rough bark pulled the thing off, but he could still feel the spot where it had been. The cold water soothed it.

He heaved his wet body, over three hundred pounds by then, out of the water. He shook and huffed and moved up onto the land, a branch snapping under his weight. The pine needles crunched underfoot. His body was much larger than it had been just a few months before. He had something like pride about the way the fat rippled over his muscle.

He climbed up the bank on the east side of the island. He walked across to the first campsite. It was open, an easy place to be. He inspected the metal grill that had been left on top of where a fire had been. There was marshmallow residue on the grates. As he licked, he found a small piece of hot dog.

The year before, he hadn't stopped on the island like this. He had walked through the clearing of the same campsite but found nothing of interest. He ate a few acorns, but it hadn't been a good year for them. Instead of lingering, he kept going across the row of campsites, travelling along the length of the island. He followed the same route as most people would go, the path of least resistance being the same for a bear. Bates Island formed a kind of land bridge. There was a clutch of oak trees on the other side. He wanted to check on their acorns.

If he didn't use the island to cross Opeongo Lake, he would have three options to get to the other side. He could swim across the middle. He could do this fairly easily, but didn't for similar reasons that a human might not. The lake was large and it took energy to get across. This was made worse when the winds picked up. The current could be pushy.

Walking was an easier way to get to the other side of the lake. The shorter route went around the south end, but the outfitting store was there. People collected in that area, which posed a risk. The other way around was to the north, but it was a long way, far enough to take a day or two. Going across the island, given its long and thin shape, was the most attractive way.

The bear stopped to nose around and sniff. He dug up a few roots that had been overlooked by the last bear who travelled over the island. He noted how long ago. He found a rotting stump, which still had some old larvae. There were acorns around too. Many more than he expected, given how thin they'd been on the ground the year before, when an early frost had nipped off many of the buds. He ate and dug in to spend the night.

The island was a nice place to be, and so he stayed. The natural foods were good, but so were the scraps he kept finding in the campsites after the busy summer. The nights grew a little colder. Some of the leaves on the deciduous trees were turning, their chlorophyll spent, and the same cues made his mind turn toward the winter. He thought about the den he had dug the previous year. It had been a good spot to spend the winter. If he continued to the west side of the lake, it wasn't far. He had a nice layer of fat, though he always wanted more. The clouds lowered. The air tightened.

And then he heard a sound. The lake had been empty. He had watched one boat, a silent canoe, slide by a few days earlier, but that was it. This boat pointed to the quiet side of the island, to the east, and started coming closer.

Soon, the motor stopped. He heard voices, one higher, one lower. He could smell humans, their food, and the oil from the fish. He was at the height of land, along the spine, and knew exactly where the activity came from.

He crept in silence, staying low, through the thicker brush to take a look.

Part Ten

WHEN TO FIGHT

26.

I WAS TRYING TO put cancer and bears behind me, but I still had a permit to spend the October long weekend in the back-country of Algonquin Park. When the weekend came around on the calendar, I decided to go. I could probably find ways to stay out of the sun. I was strong enough to paddle. I hadn't been out in the backcountry since my operation, but I didn't think the few miles would be a problem. Under the scars, the muscles on my back had strengthened.

Dave was relieved that I wanted to go, because it sounded like something the old me would want to do. He hesitated when I told him why.

I wanted to spend the night where the couple had planned to camp. I wanted to feel the temperature of the water in October. I wanted to see the position of the sun in the afternoon and how quickly it became dark in the evening. I wondered how many warm clothes I needed to bring when I went camping that late in the fall. Every year is different, but most years the leaves would be already turning and have reached peak colour by the Thanksgiving weekend. I knew the early sunset would cast the light in a slant, but I wanted to see the darkness of the shadows between the trees.

"Will the island feel haunted?" Dave asked.

I said no. I had accounted for the reality. I'd spent so much time thinking about that evening, and what happened, that there was no need for fantastic explanations. The people and the bear, in my mind, were much more than ghosts.

Maybe part of me had not quit the investigation after all.

Dave and I drove north on Friday morning. It was Canadian Thanksgiving. The boys and the dog stayed with my mom. Our sad plants were watered in advance of our departure. We took Highway 400, the main road that cuts due north. The trees sharpened at the tips. The traffic became sparse. Our car tunnelled through blasted rock. At Huntsville, we turned right onto Highway 60. We found the sign for Opeongo Lake, turned left, and our car bumped along the narrow road.

We rented a canoe and left the dock at Algonquin Outfitters around 4:30 p.m. The sun was still high and would set at 6:34 p.m. that day.

I took the stern, the back seat of the canoe. I put the bear barrel with our food in the back to better distribute our weight. As we pushed off from the dock, I used the strength of Dave's pull to control the boat with an efficient J-stroke. Soon we had the boat travelling in a graceful line toward the island. With a light load and no kids, it would only take around twenty minutes.

We were quiet as we paddled. We left any noise of the store and the dock behind. I watched the blade of my paddle slice through the water, as I have so many times. It's hypnotic. The water showed the impression of the tiny adjustments to my stroke, the deep curl that comes after a bend of my left hand. The pooling twist of the blade was further guided by my right palm on the top of the paddle. Being in a canoe is such a large part of my existence. It's been so much more than a way to travel; it's the way I've met some of my best friends, claimed my strength, and defined my life.

The sun glinted off the water and reflected up into my face. The canoe itself was aluminum. I had the UV light monitor on my phone. The count was low at that time of year and that time of day, but the app didn't know I was on a lake. It roughly doubles the amount of exposure. I wore a big hat, sunscreen, long sleeves, and pants.

Dave turned and saw the reflection of the water dapple on my chin. "It's like being on a mirror," he said.

I knew this was probably my last canoe trip, or that at the very least I needed to keep them short. Dave knew this too, but neither of us could bring ourselves to say it out loud.

As we paddled out, we talked about the couple. Dave asked if they had had a similar kind of day. I told him everything I knew about the conditions. I could say for certain that they were surrounded by the same incredible beauty. The water rolled gently under the boat. The leaves were turning, a blend of golds, reds, and oranges, colours that seemed as if they came from the heart of the land. The trees rose and fell along the ridges. There were thousands upon thousands of them running on the land beside us, their tips reaching up, swaying together. The water stretched out, a silky tension on the surface.

The silence was only broken by the call of a raven—the kenning, *swan-of-blood.*

It was still difficult to imagine violence in this setting. There were few people around. I think there were one or two other parties camping, but most of the people we saw were out for day trips. They were headed in the opposite direction, passing us on their way back in to the store. The park was even emptier in 1991. There were about half the number of people visiting every year. I could imagine how it must have felt as if there was no one else around.

As we paddled closer, I asked Dave, "Do you want to stay at another campsite?"

I had been through Opeongo many times during the summer in the years before. The campsites on the east side of the lake were usually taken first. They had the best view of the sunset and that was considered prime real estate. I explained this to Dave with a long story about how I'd always come later in the day and had never been able to grab one of those sites first. Now they were empty. It seemed like the perfect chance.

I wasn't being completely honest when I suggested this last-minute change. The truth was that I was quietly second-guessing what we were doing. The sadness I'd first felt for the couple turned, slowly, into something scarier. I felt a prickle along my back and neck. I dipped my blade in the water and stopped paddling. I let the canoe hang in the water. Dave only needed to hear the sound of my voice to know that something was up.

"Why are you changing your mind?" he asked, turning in the bow to look at me.

I wasn't sure. What was making me hesitate? It was something about how the couple must have felt that scared me.

And then, in the next moment, I knew exactly how they likely felt. Fine.

When Ray and Carola were at this point in their trip, in the motorboat, cold wind whipping, they came around the bend, angling for the island. They were most likely looking forward to the weekend and glad to be there. I doubted that they were scared at all. They couldn't see the direction danger would come from. There is a freedom afforded by not knowing what lies in your future. No statistic could help them guess what would happen next.

If they felt fine, how does a reasonable person go about trying to stay safe? As I sat in the canoe, I felt bare. I wore a life jacket, not chain mail. As a sword, my paddle wouldn't really do. The edges were rounded and sanded. It wasn't heavy. It would splinter and break easily. I looked back in the direction we had come from. A big part of me wanted to turn back, paddle to the dock, pull the boat out, and get in the car. I wanted to keep any terror separate from my life.

Being there, it laid my thinking bare. If I believed there was danger on the island, then there was a clear way to reduce the risk to my life: I could call off the trip and leave. Doing so would feel good, like there was a step I could take to help feel safe.

I could see the reality more clearly. I wasn't going to be attacked by a bear. I was more likely to drown or be stung by a bee. Even those means of death weren't statistically likely compared with the odds I faced. The danger lay much closer. The same cells that helped me paddle and kept me alive were also the ones that might kill me. Terror, if I wanted to pinpoint it, already lived inside me.

And so does the beauty of Algonquin Park. Terror and beauty can't be pulled apart. They can't be separated, no matter how tempting it might be to try.

The sun lowered over the ridge beyond the lake. It was lined with trees, the colours spread far and wide. Granite rocks climbed gracefully out of the fresh water. Trees watched us from their places on the ridges, their leaves bursting with golds, reds, oranges. As the sun lowered toward the water, the light caught me directly in the eye.

If I wanted to fight something, there was my opponent. The sunlight. My monster. But this was a battle I would never win. I was no match. The sun, the most powerful force on our planet, had already secured a victory.

Sleep-of-the-sword, a kenning for a death. It holds the idea of surrender.

I pulled the blade of my paddle in small figure eights to hold us in place. I looked back at the island again, and that's when it struck me. I could see something I hadn't been able to imagine before. And it had to do with the position of the sun.

The sun was sliding down the side of the sky directly across from the island. By then it was about an hour and a half before it would set. Dan Strickland, the park naturalist in 1991, had said something about the couple just after the attack. He intended to convey the idea that they had done nothing to bring the attack on. "They may simply have been in the wrong place at the wrong time."

So many times, I'd wondered if this was true. I'd tested many other theories and dismissed them all and had come to agree with Strickland's statement.

But then I saw that maybe his suggestion wasn't completely right either. I saw that it was possible they weren't in the wrong place at all.

When the sun went down, the angle of the thin strip of pebbled beach was at a specific aspect. I could only have noticed it while sitting in the same place on the water at close to the same time, in mid-October. It seemed that Ray and Carola might have made a deliberate decision. They wanted to watch the sunset. At this time of year, they chose the perfect campsite to catch the most spectacular view.

The couple may have been exactly where they wanted to be.

27.

FROM THE EVIDENCE, IT looked as though Carola had been cooking near the campfire when the bear entered the campsite. She was attacked first. She was most likely killed instantly with a blow to the back of the neck. The bear probably approached her from behind.

What could she have done to fight for her life?

The bear was over 300 pounds and full of muscle. A bear this size would be about five times stronger than a human of the same size. He would have a bite force of 800 pounds per square inch and his swipe could potentially have a force of up to 560 pounds.

The back of a human neck is vulnerable. Even if wearing a pack, or if given time to clasp your hands around your neck, a person approached from behind with force stands little chance.

If a bear has hunted a moose calf successfully, he could have a similar success when hunting a human. A young calf, who is not yet fully grown, and an adult human are a similar size. Both have four long limbs and a narrow body. At a glance, there may be a rough comparison to make. The bigger difference lies in what the human doesn't have standing by her side—a ferocious mother with sharp hooves.

LAURA DARBY WAS IN a similar situation. She was doing fieldwork ninety-five miles north of Thunder Bay, Ontario. Many people in Canada would tell you this is the far north, but if you look at a map of Ontario, it's not quite halfway to the top. Laura was working as a wildlife analyst and went into the bush with a co-worker, Dan Morrison. He had gone off to do fieldwork in another direction.

Laura saw a black bear running toward her at an angle. She knew black bears, and at first she assumed she wasn't his target. The bear charged right past her. But then the bear circled around and started coming toward her again. Laura yelled to make sure the bear knew she was a human. "Whoa, bear."

The bear kept coming. Laura tried to make sense of what was happening. She looked behind the bear to see if another animal had scared it. Maybe the bear was being chased? It seemed like the only reasonable explanation.

He charged past her once more and stopped, then turned toward her again. That's when she knew she was in trouble. She had bear training. She recognized the behaviour of a predatory bear. "It's hunting me," she thought.

Laura is about five foot four. She has brown hair and defined features. She moves with deliberate motions and speaks deliberately too. She doesn't rush and chooses her words precisely. Her mind works in the way of a scientist. She gives measurements of how far away from her the bear was at various points in the story. She shows me the distance with her hands, but before continuing, she double-checks the distance with her eyes, as if comparing it with her memory. She wants to tell the story accurately.

She had a radio and a clipboard in her hand. She yelled into the radio to let Morrison know she was in trouble, but she wasn't sure if the call went through. She tried to keep the clipboard in front of her; it was flimsy but better than nothing. The bear started coming again. He closed the amount of space between them. She moved behind a tree stump for some protection, though it didn't provide much. It was old and rotting. The bear started pawing it and knocked off chunks.

"Nothing will hold it back," she thought.

After moving around the rotting tree stump, the bear charged at Laura. She describes the speed as "lightning." It went from one side of her to the other, all the movement blurred. The clipboard went flying. So did her radio. It was her only link to Morrison and any other human contact.

Then the bear was on top of her.

Laura describes what happened in the next few minutes in the most admirable way. She held on to a sense of calm. She was conscious of wanting to appear in control of the situation. She didn't want it to seem that she was losing, even if she was.

"I was thinking thoughts, while my body was just doing its own thing," she tells me.

She remembers hearing herself screaming, she was kicking and fighting back, but her mind was processing what was happening. She became like a witness to her own mauling.

"I've just been bitten by a bear," she thought. "It really hurts."

She describes a feeling like awe, but she also understood the reality.

IT MAY SEEM ODD that this kind of separated thinking occurs in the middle of a traumatic event, especially when your life is in danger. But many survivors of extreme situations, whether an animal attack or a mountaineering accident, or a soldier in war, describe the experience of a split mind.

Joe Simpson, in his book *Touching the Void*, tells how he survived after falling. When his climbing partner, Simon Yates, cut his climbing rope out of necessity, Joe fell into a large crevasse on Siula Grande in the Peruvian Andes. His leg was badly broken. Against all odds, he made it out of the crevasse and started a long journey back to their camp. It would take him days, and he was aware that Simon would likely assume he was dead and leave. But something inside Joe took over and started directing him. He called it "the voice," a commanding presence that he soon let take over.

"The voice told me exactly how to go about it, and I obeyed while my other mind jumped abstractedly from one idea to another." Joe was severely dehydrated, had frostbitten fingers, and dragged a mangled leg, but he managed to hop and slide along a glacier. He had to stop sometimes to rest. "Then the voice would tell me I was late, and I would wake with a start and crawl again." Joe credits the voice with saving his life, as if it were a separate being. The voice, though, came from him.

A man who jumped off the Golden Gate Bridge in San Francisco describes an outside voice giving guidance. "I still see my hands coming off the railing," Ken Baldwin told the *New Yorker* about his jump in 1985. He was twenty-eight years old at the time and severely depressed, but had a sudden breakthrough. "I instantly realized that everything in my life that I'd thought was unfixable was totally fixable—except for having just jumped."

Baldwin lived. The experience changed his life. He came to terms with his depression and learned to manage it.

In *The Third Man Factor: The Secret to Survival in Extreme Environments*, John Geiger writes about the tricks that stressed minds are capable of playing. When the author was young, only seven years old, he saw a rattlesnake. The snake moved between Geiger and his father. He remembers his mind detaching from the immediate situation. He could survey the scene from a distance. He turned into someone who was experiencing and observing at the same time. "I was two people . . . Time seemed to slow."

Geiger goes on to speculate that the hemispheres of the brain can shift and produce the feeling of a split, a helpful presence or a muse that helps a person in an extreme situation cope with stress and remain functional.

Laura was able to process what was happening, react physically, and simultaneously keep a part of her brain allocated for strategic thinking. She consciously took defensive actions, kicking, punching, and screaming. The bear bit her leg. He started to chew on her right arm. She tried to pry open his jaws in an attempt to make him let go of her. She remembers trying to jab his eyes. "It was hard to get my fingers in."

The bear had pulled down the vest Laura wore. She wanted to protect her vital organs and her spine. She flipped over onto her stomach. The bear stood over her. He chewed on her right arm. She locked her fingers around her head to cover the back of her neck.

It turned into a game, like cat and mouse. Every bear has a different approach; this bear would grab her and shake. She started to feel smaller and smaller, like a toy getting tossed around. The bear was so much stronger, but she stayed aware and watched him closely. She didn't want to get taken farther into the woods. The bear took hold of her and shook her violently. She realized her arms weren't moving as well as they had before. Much of the muscle had been ripped.

By this point in the attack, Laura had one remaining tool at her disposal. She wore steel-toe boots. She used them as she tried to grab at a log to stop the bear from dragging her deeper into the trees.

At some point around then, she heard her co-worker, Dan Morrison, calling. He had heard her distress call after all. She rolled and shouted back to Dan as loudly as she could. The bear immediately reacted. He picked her up in his jaws and shook, whacking her head against a tree. She heard snapping. It sounded like her bones were breaking. The bear put his paw on her head and slammed it to the ground.

Laura started to feel her energy draining. She lay on her stomach, face to the ground, arms covering the back of her neck, and could feel the bear pausing too. He sat on her back, waiting for her next move. His snout was right by her neck. She could feel hot breath on her cheek; he was breathing hard, also feeling the length of the fight. She remembers taking a strange kind of comfort from this. "At least I'm not the only one that's exhausted by this," she thought.

By then Laura had started to feel the damage done to her body. Her arms were chewed up to the point where they were getting hard to control. She could hear Dan yelling and screaming. The bear grabbed her and pulled her along so easily.

Dan later told Laura that he remembered seeing a bear on top of her. Neither of them knows exactly what happened next. It is as if that part of the film was cut out, a deleted memory, and then Dan was standing between her and the bear.

The bear charged Dan four times. He had a knife, but the blade was only four inches long. It would have been too small even in lesser circumstances. In this case, though, it combined with Dan's behaviour and aggression to serve as enough of a deterrent. He held out the knife and tried to pierce the bear with it.

For the bear, the mental calculation shifted now that there were two people and a knife. This was no longer worth the calories it might yield. The bear backed off. He stayed close, though, watching them for a while. They were never exactly sure when he left. The departure was as silent as his approach had been.

They had already radioed for help. A helicopter came to evacuate them, and they were flown out. Laura lived, but only after a fight. I am sure this was because of her persistence and determination. Dan had showed up just in time.

Every bear will calculate the worth of taking a risk differently. Laura, helped by Dan, was able to tip the equation, but it was never a certainty. Around sharp teeth and claws, delicate arteries and spinal cords are incredibly vulnerable. A human body lacks armour or anything that can provide an adequate defence. The difference between life and death can be a matter of inches.

28.

RAY WAS IN THE worst kind of danger. The bear was attacking his partner. His next moves would decide if he lived or died.

The coroner, looking at Carola's injuries, thought that she died quickly from a blow to the neck. A human body has little in the way of defences against the kind of strength a bear wields. I don't think there was anything she could have done to save herself.

And for Ray, even if he was seeing clearly, if she had been struck suddenly, there may have been no way for him to know if she was unconscious, badly injured, or dead. The choices he made next show that he probably had hope.

If he was near the tent, the configuration of the main players on the campsite could be best understood as a triangle. Ray stood at the tip. On the right side was the ring of rocks around the campfire. This marked the spot where the bear attacked Carola. It's the longer side, maybe about ten good strides away from where Ray was, by the large pine tree and the tent.

From there, if Ray looked left, he would see the boat. He was up on the bank on a higher point of land. When I stood in that spot, I could have leapt to the edge of the water. It was probably around five strides away. The boat was nosed into the bank. It may or may not have been tied, but it was mostly unloaded, meaning it was lighter than when they arrived.

Ray had a clear route to the boat. The bear's attention was absorbed by another fight. He could have taken a few strides down to the beach. He would have had to undo the boat if it had been tied to the tree or a rock, and that would take one more beat. Another step and he would have the bow of the boat in hand. Maybe, using the momentum from the jump, he could have put a hand on the boat and pushed it out. The bow would have scraped into the water fairly easily. Before it floated too far, he could have climbed in.

As the boat moved away from land, he could have started the motor. A runabout is fairly stable. Even if in a panic he jumped too far or hard, the boat would stay upright. If he hadn't pushed it out far enough, his weight in the back would encourage the nose to lift from the land. The engine had been running within the last hour, or less. It barely had time to go cold. It would probably be easy to start, a pull of the cord, two at most.

The boat was a rental and, likely, had recently been serviced. They had enough gas for the weekend, and the trip out hadn't been enough to run down a standard tank. They would have at least planned to carry enough gas for the way back and, probably, for a few day trips. Ray could have grabbed the cord, ripped it, and made the motor roar. Then held the throttle and cranked it. He could have been at the store in less than ten minutes and called for help.

The bear might have had other ideas. He could have been diverted by the sounds Ray made during his escape. The sudden leap, the thump of his feet on the beach, the clang of a shoe on aluminum, or the roar of the motor—any of these things might have pulled on the bear's attention.

Chuck Fisher was the foreperson of a tree-planting crew near Hearst, Ontario, in the spring of 1992. He heard a planter on his team in distress and ran over to see what was happening. A woman had been working when she looked up to see a black bear approaching. Chuck started shouting at the bear to scare it off. The bear shifted his attention from the woman to Chuck. The bear charged. Others came running to help, but each time a new person arrived to create a distraction, the bear would turn on them and charge. This happened a few times as the crew worked together to get everyone safely into a van.

If the noises of Ray's escape had been enough to catch the bear's attention, it could have been trouble. The bear was so fast, he could have covered that distance in seconds, but he was not faster than the engine. If Ray had been in the boat and started it quickly, there had been time to get away. The boat was his route for escape.

I think Ray's choice was deliberate, given what happened next, but it put him in a difficult place. Stephen Herrero has advice for someone in Ray's position: "The unarmed person should try to escape, for example to a nearby hard-sided shelter." But there was no place like that on the island. No car, no cabin—even the privy didn't have walls. The trees were, for the most part, too mature to climb, but even if Ray had tried, a motivated bear could have pulled him out.

After deciding to stay, Ray had one last option when faced with an aggressive black bear at close range. As Herrero says, "Fight back."

Ray went toward the boat and grabbed an oar. Oars are often stored along the gunwales, or edges, of a motorboat for safety reasons. They are a way to move the boat in case the motor breaks down or you run out of gas.

Ray probably struck the bear with the oar to try to stop the attack. That may have been what caused the bear to turn on Ray and drive him back toward the water. Or the bear may have noticed Ray near the boat, stopped his attack, and turned to charge. Either way, the prints showed they ended up near the front of the campsite. The evidence left behind told what happened next.

"It was all there," Dave Stott said. "The story laid out in the sand."

That was also where the broken oar was found, on the ground near the beach.

The bear had long contusions, or bruises, "at several locations on the anterior half of the body." The anterior is the front. There was a linear bruise one centimetre wide and eight centimetres long along the top of the head, just to the side of the ridge of bone that runs lengthwise along the skull. There was also bruising around his neck and shoulders. This suggests, though doesn't prove conclusively, that the bear turned toward the person with the oar. He was hit head-on.

It matters that it was an oar, not a paddle, because of the kind of weapon it makes. A paddle is used in a canoe. It tends to be lighter, only about two pounds, as it's held in the hands. Oars are heavier. They can weigh five pounds or more. When they are being used, oars sit in a lock and are pulled for leverage. They are not made for subtlety, but to pull as much water as possible.

An oar is much more difficult to break. A person couldn't split the wood with their bare hands. I don't think a bear could split it easily either. That an oar broke says something about the force of the confrontation. Ray put up a real fight.

When the oar broke, it might have fallen out of Ray's hands, or been struck or ripped from them. He found himself empty-handed and must have grabbed a gas can. It was probably in the boat or, less likely, by the fire if they used some as an accelerant. Gasoline was found poured on the ground around where the fight had taken place. Also, there was gas found on the bear's hide. It seems Ray tried to douse the bear.

A lighter was also found on the ground, a plastic Bic. If Ray poured gas on the bear as a deterrent, I think he couldn't get a flame, or it failed to catch. The necropsy report on the bear lists everything found on the bear, including the distribution of the copper casing from the bullet of the police rifle. There was gas on the pelt, but there isn't any mention of singe or burn marks.

Ray's glasses were also on the ground.

There was blood on a log and through the dirt, as though something had been dragged. From there, marks in the pine needles led from where the confrontation occurred at the front of the campsite up toward the ridge where the bodies were found. There were no other human tracks made around the campsite until the search party arrived.

To survive the bear attack, Ray should have climbed into the boat and motored off, but he didn't. He stayed.

Part Eleven

A TIME TO SURRENDER

29.

DAVE AND I DID stay at the campsite where the attack took place. The Friday evening we spent on Bates Island was uneventful. Or, the events that took place were within the range of things I'd expect. As we were setting up camp, a motorboat came around the bend and passed by on the west side of the island. It was a water taxi, like the one Jerry had driven me out to the island in a month earlier. It had a bigger engine than the couple had on their runabout, but any engine was loud in that setting. I stopped and listened and realized I would have heard it from any position on the island. There was no way to miss it. A bear would hear it too. There was no doubt in my mind, the bear wasn't startled. He heard their boat when the couple approached the island.

I started the fire and boiled water. Dave put up the tent. I took our sleeping bags out of our waterproof dry bags and laid them out because the night was clear. Dave made an amazing dinner, pasta, pesto, and cheese. We ate chocolate and watched the sunset. I sat between his legs and leaned my head against his chest. He put his warm fingers against the skin of my neck. We had the perfect view.

I put on my puffy winter coat. The moon was almost full, and we stayed up to watch its light send shadows through the trees and across the campsite. The heavy scent of the pine moved closer to the ground, the cooling air holding it down. The stars were bright. The sky had no edge. Underneath it, silence rang across the black water.

We managed to stay up until 8 p.m. When it became too cold, we crawled into the tent.

"If a bear comes," said Dave in the pitch black, "you're the one who is getting up."

I agreed that was fair enough. And then I woke up in the middle of the night. Did I hear something?

I held my breath and listened. It happened again, something brushing against the fabric of the tent. Then a snap. My eyes opened wide. I tuned in and listened. After a few minutes, I heard it again. It came as a thump and then a swish. Something hit the nylon fly and brushed. In the moonlight, I caught a glimpse of movement from the corner of my eye.

I did what I always do, forced myself to get up, unzip the tent, and look. Dave was now wide awake and, with a tight voice, asked what I'd heard.

A few years before, we had been sitting on the porch of a cottage in Georgian Bay. We were drinking a beer and chatting when I stopped, looked out, and said, "I smell a bear." Dave didn't believe me at first, but we scanned the brush and I saw branches twitching. Soon we could see the small, round back of a black bear about a hundred feet off. Ever since, Dave has assumed I have some kind of dark superpower.

The truth is simpler. Black bears have a distinct, musky smell. I've never heard it described the same way twice, but dirty feet, wet leaves, and a big wet dog come to mind.

I heard the sound again and looked in the direction it came from. We had pitched our tent under an old pine tree. In the moonlight, I watched a large clump of needles fall from a branch. They dropped against the fly and made the same sound I had heard before.

I reported to Dave that we were under attack by clumps of pine needles. They might sound terrifying, but were unlikely to cause much damage. We'd live.

Still, it felt significant in the morning to wake up, unzip the tent, and look out at the lake. Something had shifted from the night before. I was struck by how much had changed in the last year. I had booked this trip in hopes of meeting up with my old self again, but that didn't happen. The person I recognized, the one who would have waited for the sun to become strong, paddled out into the open, dove into the freezing water, and lain on a warm rock to let the sun dry my skin, she was gone. I'd never find her again.

But then, waking up to this kind of view was something I had experienced for much of my life. Everything had changed and stayed exactly the same. Algonquin Park was older and had existed far longer than me. The land would keep on holding these patterns, the ripples on the lake, the sway of the trees, the angled morning light. Long after I was gone, all this would remain.

After Beowulf defeated Grendel's mother, he reigned over his land for fifty years. There was a great calm before the fire-breathing dragon came. The old warrior must have woken up every day and felt glad to see the land around him quiet for such a long time.

OUR KINGDOM AT THE campsite wasn't quite as peaceful that morning. We had bought decaffeinated coffee by mistake. It was my turn to nearly panic, but we made it and managed to struggle through a cup or two. It wasn't all that bad.

As always, while drinking coffee, Dave and I started talking about the canoe routes we wanted to do. We pulled out a map. He put a finger on a set of lines that traced around the park. They weren't on the blue-coloured paper, which showed the contours of reflective water, but on the green in the trees. There were hiking trails that went through the park in every direction, and most were covered by the canopy. I'd seen these trails when I was out before but never really taken them in. They climbed up ridges, went past lakes and through the shallow valleys, all this under the great canopy of the trees. The map was pointing us toward the shade.

I had never explored the backcountry of the park by foot. We talked about how we could get miles in early, take a break in the middle of the day, when the sun is the highest, then get going again toward the evening. This was a far safer way for me to be in the wilderness. Before my eyes, the park opened back up.

"This isn't your last canoe trip," he said. "It's the first day we start backcountry hiking."

After that, Dave started asking about the details of the attack. He knew I'd been out to the island earlier in the year, and I'd told him some of what I'd found, but when I'd brought it up the night before, he wasn't interested. This morning he confessed that, after successfully surviving the night, now seemed like the better time to be curious.

I showed him where the couple's boat was pulled onto the beach and what the scene was like. I pointed to the spot where the tent was set up, mentioned how the sleeping bags were wrapped and the groceries were still being carried up. Dave stood at the front of the campsite and commented on how close the campsite was to the mainland on the east side.

I showed Dave where the oar was found. A *sea-thrower*.

We followed the line where I had walked with Jerry. I made drag marks with my foot through the pine needles to show how they looked. We went back to where the bodies were found. Dave commented on how far the bear went to get to the back of the campsite. He was right. It was a significant distance and uphill, especially dragging an adult human body. A body is heavy, and there were two. Even though the bear was larger, it would have been hard work. I hadn't really thought of it before, but the island was otherwise empty. There must have been a specific reason the bear wanted to get them up there.

There was a distinct ring of flattened earth in a semicircle around the beach that marked the boundaries of the camp. It reached back about thirty feet. Beyond that, the balsams and shrubs started to grow again. There was a marked difference between where the humans walked and where they stopped, as if we had all silently agreed to mark our territory with a boundary. There must have been hundreds of people who had stayed at the campsite during the busy summer, and most abided by these borders.

We walked to the back of the site, where the bodies had been cached. It was clear the bear knew this boundary too. He had moved the bodies up and over an edge. There was a slight hill, a ridge in the earth, and he pulled them behind it. It seemed purposeful. He knew where humans went. He knew where they didn't. He chose a spot where he was likely to be hidden and have less chance of interruption. He had made a cache beyond where humans tend to roam at a quieter time of year.

I started to appreciate the extent to which bears study humans and understand our patterns. I thought about the cinnamon bear in my tree-planting camp and how much she worked with or against our movements. She learned how to break into vans, open backpacks, and peel the lid off Tupperware. She knew our days off. Maybe she hadn't managed to get her hands on a tube of toothpaste before, but when she did get a whiff, it was interesting. She went to great lengths to shred my friend's tent to investigate.

In the same way, this bear worked around, and with, the human use of the campsite. There is a strong connection between our two species. If research points toward how we might share levels of intelligence and a similar kind of robust social life, the campsite seemed to be a kind of proof of this in action.

We had a quiet moment to pay our respects to Ray and Carola. I placed two round rocks, shiny and smoothed by the water, near where the remains were found. It was a small way to mark their memory.

Dave wanted to get breakfast going. I told him I'd be down in a minute because I wanted to look around a little more.

I stood where the brush was grown in just enough to give me cover. The slight ridge provided the perfect shelter to crouch behind. I knelt down and looked at the campfire ring from there. I could see the water. The thin strip of beach was tucked under the bank, but our canoe sat in plain sight where we had dragged it up the beach. The spot where we had made dinner and sat by the fire was in my direct line of vision. This was where the bear had been. He had watched them. Part of me could see as he did.

Dave's back was now a blue oval, his Gore-Tex jacket clearly visible. He crouched over our Coleman stove and, at this distance, looked smaller than I usually think of him. A second person would be similarly visible, moving around over to the side, with the tent, caught up in poles and thinking about unpacking the sleeping bags. I would be able to see them too.

The pieces of evidence clicked together.

I had walked that very campsite with people who arrived on the scene five days after the attack. I've read reports, talked to experts, learned about the kind of people Ray and Carola were. All these things are filtered through my experience in the park, with bears, of having cancer, and of wanting to survive. The past and present are in constant conversation with each other.

There were no witnesses to the attack, but at that moment, I knew what had happened. All the details that hadn't made sense for so long came together. I understood how it went.

30.

THE BEAR WAS IN the brush, low, stalking. He had heard the motor and knew people were coming. He watched as the couple climbed out of the boat to look around. There was a clear line of sight from his position to the ring of rocks around the campfire. He watched as a bag of groceries was set down.

The bear was eight and a half years old by then. He had seen many people in the park. The reasons behind their seasonal migrations were a mystery, but he spent little time on things that lay beyond his range of influence. For such a powerful animal, he had a humbling acceptance. He let their reasons be. But when it came to things that he could see, hear, smell, or lick, those were of interest.

The two people separated. It became more interesting; the glimmer of a chance appeared between them.

When he was stalking, he didn't see through the eyes of another creature. It was more like tuning into a nervous system. Where do their strengths come from and how are they vulnerable? He knew all about the necks, spines, eyes, and brains of mammals like these. One of them walked farther into the woods, a little deeper into the darkness, away from the other.

The bear tensed and licked his lips, but hesitated for a few beats of his heart. There was another campsite along the shore. He hadn't been paying attention and didn't know if others had pulled up to it. He waited for just long enough to check that it was clear.

In that time, the person walked back toward the campfire. A pang of disappointment. Caution had lost him a chance.

The two bodies stayed apart, though. One was by a tree with a tent, distracted and focused on his hands. The other was closer.

A loud hiss came from the campfire, the stove. He picked up a foot, one paw closer. Under his weight, a twig snapped. He froze. The sound of the compressed gas burning had covered for him. It sent a foggy smell into the air. Even if the people had good noses, the stink of gas provided some cover. It came toward him as encouragement.

The body near the fire stood up and bent over the bag of groceries. He took in her shape. The girth was much like a moose calf, with long, dangling limbs, but without a guardian three times the bear's weight. He didn't like to be outnumbered and usually steered clear of such situations, but two the size of moose calves seemed manageable. Their teeth were blunt, their hooves were still soft and pliable, they had no antlers, and their haunches weren't powerful. Moose calves on their own wouldn't harm him.

Of course, these weren't calves. They were people. He had spent a lifetime being wary of them. There was no discharge smell from a gun, or trace of the powdery residue that came from them, but that didn't mean anything. They could be hidden or concealed and appear by surprise. He had the glancing memory of the three men he had encountered the month before. It came as an irritation, a spark of anger, or maybe a dark smudge in the form of a grudge. Not vengeance, but resentment. It was similar to how he thought of his rival male bears with contempt.

Then one sniff told him something new had been produced. A tray of ground beef was set down on the pile of rocks. His nostrils twitched. Raw meat, and the tray had a sluice of blood running under it.

The smell of the red meat sent a stab of hunger through him. It pumped from his heart and through his veins. From there, the feeling found the lining of his stomach and lodged into his centre. It was more than hunger. It was a drive that he wouldn't act on until the spring, but it had already come and settled inside him. A craving for sex. The iron content of meat, the slight metallic tang, triggered the feeling.

By the spring, he would become ravenous. He would go to great lengths, including risking his life, to satisfy his urges. But not yet. In this moment it was more of a gnawing feeling, a distant longing, but something deep that he knew well.

His mental calculus didn't play out in thoughts or words, but rather through his eight years of experience, through his instincts, and through his impulses, inherited from all the bears that came before. These filtered through what he saw before him. Light came through the trees, lowering, flattening. Time pressed down against him. He hunted best in the day.

The man by the tent wasn't much larger than a young bear. The bear thought of the kill site with the carcass of the deer. When challenged, how easily his tooth had sliced through the immature hide. It took one bite, only half-serious, around the neck to make the young thing yelp and run off. The memory of that came with a flush of blood, the large mouthfuls of intestines and blood that came after. The deer had minced between his molars, slid down his throat, and become part of him. The bodies he ate became his own. They made energy run through his blood and were the strength of his bone.

He looked back to the body by the ring of rocks. Not that he had a measure, but that much meat could provide between 125,000 and 150,000 calories. That bulk would be added to his. He had done well that year. He was one of the largest bears in the park. But he hadn't got there by being easily satisfied. All that had come before taught him to be bold. Many of the chances he'd taken had paid off.

Around him, the leaves were turning. Soon it would be winter. And it was this that tipped a balance inside him. He could feel the pressure of the season turning; it thrummed against the sensitive ridge of his gums, it beat like a drum against the pad of his nose, it rang like a persistent sound in his ears. Under his weight, the pads of his paws itched with it.

From all sides, the change of season presses against an animal that will soon go down for a long winter nap. The ground would freeze. Snow would cover the remaining berries. Ice would lock the fish away. The cold would hold in the smell of all that was eatable. He would go to sleep not because he wanted to, but because there wasn't enough to eat. To stay alive, he had to have a way of burning less energy.

And, come spring, his life would hang on whatever energy he had managed to conserve over the long winter. His best hope for success was a little extra padding going in. Here, before him, was one last chance to bulk up and thrive.

AS DAN STRICKLAND, THE park naturalist in Algonquin Park in 1991, said to a camera crew, "The surprise is why more bears don't [attack people]. Human beings are small, nourishing, and available. There's usually no injury or disease in the bears that attack. They're just exceptional bears. They've taken advantage of a situation, been innovative."

The bear made a decision. He had gained enough weight to survive the winter. He wanted more. He would bulk up on meat. He would go into hibernation with more fat and muscle. In the spring, he would wake up stronger, bigger, and more able to win any disagreement over food and females. Maybe he wouldn't even have to fight. The other male bears would size him up and turn away. He would mate. He would survive.

The bear charged.

31.

RAY WAS LIVING A nightmare. Except he was awake, in the light of day, seeing it with his own eyes. If terror is fear caught on fire, I have no doubt about that part of what Ray felt. His reaction had to be physical. The heart, blood, and breath, all would spike to levels that were impossible to sustain for long. When a place switches from tranquil to horrific in an instant, unless the body goes numb, there has to be a primal physical reaction. It's the only way for the mind to follow along.

After that first rush of fear, there is a greater range of behaviours and reactions between individuals. How did he keep going? It's impossible to reach inside another person's mind. Ray is gone, but given the evidence, I don't think he continued in a state of terror. Terror is a huge feeling. It takes up so much space. It blots out everything around it. It occupies the rational faculties in a way that makes it hard to function.

Ray chose to stay and fight, but he wasn't swinging blindly. The state of the campsite in the aftermath showed that he turned his attention outwards. He was processing the scene. He may have been able to split his mind like Laura Darby, keeping up a fight with the help of a conscious narrator helping him make decisions. When one thing didn't work, he tried something else. He did this at least three times.

The more I learned about Ray and his situation, by talking to one of his friends and analyzing the evidence, the more I felt something moving inside me. Scar tissue had grown across my back, the muscles underneath changed shape, and over them stretched my reconfigured imagination. What would motivate someone to go after a three-hundred-pound bear with an oar?

No one knows what happened next. If the past is a foreign country, there is no way to travel back. There are, however, ways to read the evidence that was left behind.

To the police, there were footprints, paw prints, and drag marks that told a story of a crime. For a biologist, there was a story of food sources, den sites, and a coming hibernation. To a pathologist, the evidence came from injuries on bodies, long bruises, trauma to the neck, and contusions.

As a writer, I combined these stories from experts with interviews, memories, photos, and my own reading. When I took them together, I remembered why I write fiction. The best stories may be old, but they are never static. They change and adapt to fit the context they are told in. A story can't change what happened in the past, but it can offer comfort, guidance, or solace to those who are still alive. Through this story, I found my voice again.

RAY'S FIRST THOUGHT WHEN he heard an ungodly sound came in a flash. He wanted the bear off Carola. His breath came out of his mouth like a huff and maybe like a chant, *off, off, off.* He couldn't hear his own voice for all the blood rushing past his ears. His mind flashed to the bear he'd seen at the campsite years before. It had been small in comparison, and it ripped the lid off the privy. The lid had been four feet in length and two feet wide, reinforced with planks running across the back, and still, the wood had splintered like toothpicks. He didn't think about the strength of a bear, not exactly, but that image, splitting wood, came to him by way of instruction—"This thing could snap me." He needed a weapon.

Off, his breath rushed out, hand on the rough bark of the pine, as he jumped down to the pebbled beach. The rubber of his soles took the brunt, but he didn't feel the landing. A hand on the boat. Inside his chest, his heart pumped hard. His pupils were dilated, his nostrils flaring, and his breath coming fast.

That rush of blood was love. It flooded through his body as a strength—a force strong enough to act as a counterweight to danger. He didn't think of getting in the boat. He would never have left the island.

It was just *off, off, off,* and his hand was on the gunnel, the oar. He didn't make a decision to grab it. A hand was on the shaft and he knew that was right. It lay under the edge of the boat, along the length, held in a clip. He pried one end. It fell loose.

Heavier than expected, the blade was pointed toward the back of the boat. The end thumped against the hull. *Bang.* When the blade hit, the reverberation against the aluminum boat sounded like a tin drum, hollow and drawn, but he didn't take this in. All he could hear was wet lungs, snarling, from the campsite behind him. The oar was in his hands, a firm grip, fingers wrapped; he didn't feel the weight. He pivoted on his back foot and scrambled to the roots and up the bank.

The bear turned in a flash, his muscles bunched and curling.

Ray never thought for a second that this might be a false charge or that the bear was bluffing. The bear's intention was clear, the anger shot through the tension of his body, ears flat, mouth open with teeth exposed. The nervous system carried it from one body to the next.

Ray had a moment, the length of one half breath, to steady himself. He splayed his feet wide. He brought the oar overhead. As soon as his arms were lengthened as far as they would go up to the sky, he yelled, a hoarse cry, the sound raw and uneven, but no one heard it. With both hands, he brought the length of the oar down. He wasn't aiming so much as using every muscle in his body to slam it.

A dull thump. The length of the oar went along the bear's head, connecting with the skull. The bear stopped, stunned and dazed. Their breath—the bear's, the man's—heaved in and out at the same time. The bear staggered, a step to the side.

Maybe Ray was able to see Carola and wanted to get closer. If gravity pulled on that campsite, she was at the centre.

He needed to get around the bear. His feet were in the dirt, oar in his hand. He lifted his head to bring it up again, but something was wrong. It went dark, black, with no horizon. The force didn't feel like a body. There was no give, no softness, nothing vulnerable, no edges. It slammed into him like a wall. The impact knocked him down. The back of his head hit a root, but that didn't register.

The bear was on him. A tooth went through his skin and he could feel it lodge in his right bicep. And then he looked down at his hand, which held tightly to the broken end of the oar. It was split in two pieces. He held the splintered end up like a sword. He brought it in to jab as hard as he could. This pulled the bear's attention to the side. The snapping jaws went for the wood to stop the irritation from that direction.

It was just enough to shift the bear's weight. Ray rolled to the side and turned, scrambling. And a voice came to him. The words were sharp and commanding, and they told him to get something, anything, and at the same time another voice made an observation. *Oh, is this how you are going to die?* It almost made him laugh, the way it was asked. The answer was yes. He knew it then, but instead of that being a reason to give up, it charged him.

He was back at the boat, grabbing the can of gas. How did he find the lighter? Maybe in a pocket, but it was there in his hand and he turned with it. An ungodly grunt, this time from Ray. His molars clenched. He had no hope for either of them, not a shard or a glimmer. Living didn't matter. He'd felt the power of the bear and knew there was no chance to counter it.

Most people would have given up. Ray undoubtedly fought through pain and injury. He kept trying. The gas splashed. It chugged onto the ground, on the dirt, spilling through the pine needles. The noxious stench of it filled his head, a light, airy feeling, as he watched his thumb slide against the rough wheel of the lighter. It struck the red pad. Nothing happened, and he thought without a trace of panic, almost a laugh, "These things always let me down."

He flicked the lighter once more, but it didn't light. Only his left hand was working now, and it had always been the clumsier one. The right sat limp by his side. A connection lost. He dropped the lighter.

Maybe he slumped down then. Maybe no words came out of his mouth, but he did not doubt that his feeling travelled in her direction. The wounds open, nerves raw, words weren't needed anymore. A thought could travel from one mind to the next through the network that lay open, skin to skin, bones pulling the meaning along. Maybe he knew that on some level, she could feel him fighting to be closer. Maybe she knew she wasn't alone.

WHEN IT'S MY TURN to fight, I hope to be as brave as Ray.

Part Twelve

HOW TO LIVE

32.

IN THE AFTERMATH OF the Bates Island attack, a columnist collected what she called a "rash" of bear incidents. She listed a series of encounters that had happened in the years leading up to 1991. A student collecting soil samples in northern Ontario was attacked and killed by a black bear, two hunters were attacked not far away, and a hiker was killed in Montana's Glacier Park after startling a grizzly sow and her cubs. Another hiker was killed in Jasper National Park in Alberta. Two men from Seattle were attacked on a trip through British Columbia. "Bears are," the columnist wrote, "wandering from New Jersey across the George Washington Bridge into Manhattan."

When traumatic events catch the public's attention, it's understandable that one reaction to fear is to grasp at patterns. As humans, we have less control over our surroundings than we'd like. Putting an order to things, finding a pattern, is an attempt to predict what happens next. With hindsight, there are more rational explanations for these incidents than a bear invasion.

A recent cluster of attacks in 2021 prompted a fresh worry that the bears were turning on us.

By looking closely at what happened on Bates Island, by understanding what motivated the bear, I start to see a different kind of story. More than a million people go through Algonquin Park every year. Opeongo Lake is one of the busiest access points. Ontario has the second-largest black bear population in North America. They do well in habitats where people thrive. The black bear population is growing. Our population is growing too.

Stephen Herrero's paper, published in 2011, establishes a positive linear relationship between the number of fatal black bear attacks per decade and the human population size in the United States and Canada per decade. "It's not an increase in hungry bears," said Herrero. "It's simply more and more people out there interacting with bears."

After a traumatic event, we look for patterns in individual behaviour too. There can be intense focus on the victims, their actions, thoughts, and reactions. I had this response to the Bates Island attack myself. My search for information started from a primal need to survive. I wanted to identify a mistake the couple made. Did they mishandle their food, attract the bear, or were they not prepared? If I could identify a mistake, then all I had to do was not repeat it—that might keep me safe. Grasping for fault was an attempt to isolate myself from tragic circumstances.

Similarly, I wanted to hear that this attack happened because the bear was sick, a rogue, or a monster gone out of his mind. By trying to move beyond these simplistic predator–prey dynamics, I now appreciate how an attack might have played out from a bear's perspective.

In a letter to the editor of a Sudbury newspaper, Mike Commito wrote about the aftermath of the Bates Island attack. He worried that all the emphasis on the rarity of the attack, the small chance that it could happen again, was an attempt to calm the public. The victims, he said, are not statistics. "They were people, with families, and their names should be included in a discussion of black bear fatalities."

As Raymond Jakubauskas and Carola Frehe can no longer speak for themselves, I wanted to hear from family and friends who loved them.

Regan Martin grew up with Ray. Regan described Ray as quiet and unassuming, but he had a strength of character and a fortitude that most people around him recognized. When something needed to get done, he was the one who stepped up.

The two boys were inseparable through their school days. They lived about two blocks from each other in the west end of Toronto. Ray's house was close to the railway tracks. "One afternoon on the way home, a blizzard started and, parka hoods up, we were walking backwards along the tracks and against the wind. Sounds kind of silly, no? Sure enough, I thought I heard something and turned around to see the headlights of a train coming straight toward us. I froze and would definitely have been run down were it not for Ray grabbing me by the parka and yanking me off the tracks to have the two of us fall in a bundle to the side just as the train barrelled past at full speed. Without a doubt, he saved my life. I was in shock, yet he was calm and cool as can be."

Regan said he reminded Ray about that day many times, but Ray attributed his reaction to reflex. He joked that it would have been too difficult to break in a new best friend.

"Ray loved the outdoors," Regan said. "I like to think, despite the tragic consequences of his death, he at least died in one of the places he loved most on earth."

Ray's mother is no longer alive, but after the attack a reporter went to her house. She spoke in English, a newly acquired language, of her loss. "Now they go no more," she said.

Sven Frehe is Carola's son. He remembers how much she used to sing, "and she sang loudly in a wonderful, thick German accent with no cares." On meet-the-teacher day in school, his mom stole the show "in her tight jeans, high boots, and leather jacket. She wore it well."

Their family often went camping. They paddled on Whitefish Lake in Algonquin Park and were caught in a heavy summer thunderstorm. They enjoyed watching "the beavers swim at dusk and the view of endless wilderness from the Lookout trail."

About ten years ago, Sven rented a yurt, a canvas tent, just outside Algonquin and went to stay there with his dog. "We were alone on a very isolated lake. I am now an accomplished musician and decided to bring my euphonium to play on the dock. The sound carried for at least ten kilometres with a wonderful echo. I played all my favourite beautiful melodies with the wolves, owls, and loons providing accompaniment. On that night I thought that perhaps she could somehow hear me."

Carola lives on, in a way. She never had the chance to meet Sven's daughters, but he sees his mother's lively spirit in them.

"Grief is the price of love," he wrote.

33.

I SPOKE TO LAURA Darby about her recovery. Healing was a long process. She had to undergo a series of operations, but slowly she regained muscle strength and sensation. She described the difficulty of going on a thirty-minute hike. "I would be dead on my feet, I'd be so tired." She attributed this not to physical issues, but to elevated levels of awareness. "If I was in the bush and I heard a twig snap, I had a full-body reaction."

She went skydiving the summer after the attack. She remembers being on the plane, sitting near the door, waiting for her turn to jump, and feeling nothing. "No adrenalin whatsoever." Maybe there are no bears in the clouds, but at the same time, she recognized that life, joy, and fulfillment are based on sensation. Healing became a search for a way to align her inner landscape with the terrain around her. She went travelling, only visiting countries that didn't have bears, and put herself in new situations that weren't always comfortable. That way, she could practise responding.

Talking about what happened has helped Laura the most. Words laid the path for her healing. She has an incredible strength. As we spoke via a screen, I could feel her liveness pulsing through my computer. I kept glancing at something behind her. I couldn't quite make out what it was, a large dark object hanging on the wall.

During a pause in our conversation, I asked Laura about it. She moved the camera to show me. It was the pelt of the bear who had attacked her, now in the form of a rug. She kept it hanging on the wall in her living room.

When a bear attacks a human, they don't usually end up on someone's wall, but they *are* hunted and, if found, killed. Biologists and park staff told me they wished there was another way to deal with a problem bear, but if a predatory attack proved successful, why wouldn't the bear try again?

In the past one hundred years, about one person per year has been killed by a black bear on average, though the average number edges up after 1960. On the other hand, we kill bears in the thousands.

People are heading into the wilderness in greater numbers. Since 1991, the number of visitors to Algonquin Park has roughly doubled. In the US, in 2022, the National Park Service recorded 312 million recreational visits, which was up 5 percent from the previous year. At the same time, the black bear population is growing. Herrero found that 86 percent of fatal attacks have occurred since 1960. In the past twenty years the fatalities have increased, and the number of known fatal black bear attacks in North America has edged over seventy. With more people heading into bear country and more bears wandering out of it, more conflicts are inevitable.

LOOKING BACK TO THAT Friday in October 1991, I try to understand what might have prevented such a tragic end. The answer doesn't lie in any of Carola's or Ray's actions. They found themselves in an unfortunate circumstance. They did their best. The park was managed in the usual way. The police and emergency responders came as fast as they could and worked to the best of their ability. The attack happened because the bear made a decision—he had taken risks that paid off in the past. I can't know the bear's perspective, not exactly, but I can respect his abilities and intelligence. From there, I can imagine. A bear's decisions are driven by his stomach. He follows the food.

According to studies, the bear probably lived in a wilderness area that was smaller than his range. While looking for food, he didn't observe the borders drawn on a map. His quest for food took him to an open-pit dump. It has since been closed, but he would still be attracted to any accessible garbage or human food. Once back inside the park, he lived in a habitat open to logging. When his habitat changes, a bear adjusts his range. His borders will change.

Climate change, wildfires, and new housing developments all alter the food supply of a black bear. They need space to roam, eat, sleep, mate, and live. This is true at the individual level, and it scales to how we think about bears as a population. It may not be possible to stop all conflict with bears, but we can avoid much of it. If bears have a right to live on their terms, and have the space to do so, they are more likely to keep to themselves.

Like Algonquin Park, there are many wilderness areas in North America that aren't as protected as they might seem.

The Arctic National Wildlife Refuge in northeastern Alaska shares a border with two Canadian national parks, Ivvavik and Vuntut. These lands are the home of the Gwich'in, who call the area Iizhik Gwats'an Gwandaii Goodlit, or the Sacred Place Where Life Begins. It's an apt name because the refuge includes the birthing grounds of one of the last remaining migratory caribou herds. In the last hundred years the caribou numbers have plummeted, which has drastically changed how the Gwich'in live. There are about seven hundred species of plants and animals in the refuge. It's also estimated that it is home to more than seven billion barrels of oil. In December 2017, the Trump administration put a bill through Congress that approved oil exploration in the refuge. In 2020, a leasing program was announced to make way for widespread drilling. In 2023, President Joe Biden cancelled the leases, but it feels like a reprieve rather than anything final.

In California, an environmental non-profit filed a lawsuit in 2022 to stop what it called commercial logging in Yosemite National Park, affecting almost two thousand acres in the park. The project would have seen thousands of healthy ponderosa pines, white firs, and cedars removed. The National Park Service said the logging was part of fire risk reduction. The non-profits who launched the lawsuit questioned why a loophole was used to avoid public consultation.

In Montana, twelve square miles of forest land beside Yellowstone National Park has been designated for commercial logging. Three conservation groups have launched a lawsuit to stop the logging and the building of fifty-six miles of new roads in the area. They say that the logging will damage grizzly bear and lynx habitat. The NPS countered that the forest will regenerate in about fifteen years and that the impacts on wildlife will be "minimal."

It shouldn't have come as a surprise to learn that more than 40 percent of Algonquin Park is logged. Nor should I have been caught off guard that the First Nations people whom the park was named after were kicked out when it was formed. I've started using a different approach when trying to understand the protections around a wild place. Now I ask two questions: From what? For whom?

Our ideas about the wilderness have been shaped over time. In Canada and the US, a complex web of agencies, laws, decrees, and jurisdictions govern these areas. It's hard to compare one wilderness area with another, but many have something in common. They were formed in the traditions of colonial power, a system of political control where one people dominates another and uses their resources to extract wealth. While the players have changed, many of the mechanisms remain. The jaws of colonialism continue to chew.

There are groups who are working toward something better. A proposal in Ireland is looking to enshrine the rights of nature into the national constitution. The idea is to have trees, mountains, and rivers recognized as things that have the right to exist, be restored, and be respected. In New Zealand, Maori people fought to have the Whanganui River granted the same legal rights as a human being. In Canada, the Innu Council of Ekuanitshit and the municipal council of Minganie passed resolutions to give the Rivière Magpie, a river in Quebec, legal personhood. A river is a living thing with a right to exist. So is a bear.

THE WILDERNESS IS A network of interdependent relationships. This might sound like an unromantic view of nature, but I see the opposite. It's hopeful. Humans are the driving force in shaping the landscape. If we made the wilderness, then we can also define a better shape for it. We can do more to conserve it.

A bear attack and cancer are not alike, but when brought together, they can lend meaning. One shifted my perspective on the other. I found a way to heal in Algonquin Park; I let go of ideas that held my fear in place. Now I see the city and the wilderness as inextricably bound.

The wilderness has never been empty. It doesn't have borders. It's a word that defines a relationship between the people, the wildlife, and the land. It's ancient and will be here long after I'm gone. I can't control where or how it goes. It's under the carpet, in the alley behind my house, in the lake, inside a glacier, and on an island in Algonquin Park. It's inside the mind of a black bear.

It's also much closer. It lives in my cells. To some, those cells might have a mutation. To me, they are cells inherited from my dad. I have cancer. It's wild inside me.

34.

DURING MY INVESTIGATION, WHILE I was staying near Algonquin Park, I intended to go hiking. Something far more dramatic happened.

I set an early alarm, woke in the dark, and drove to a trailhead while the sun cracked over the horizon. It might be impossible to avoid the sun altogether, but I could lessen my exposure. In conversation with my dermatologist, I had developed a set of rules, or constraints, to manage risk. UV rays are strongest in the middle of the day, in spring and summer, and near the equator. Some tight-weave fabrics offer good protection. I installed a UV monitor on my phone. The trees in Algonquin Park provided a canopy. It was a place I could hike outside and stay relatively safe.

The quiet morning reminded me of all the times I woke up early on a trip and tiptoed out to sit by the lake. It was still. The road lay empty. The sky brightened into a smooth slab, turning into a block above my head. It seemed separate from the land, as though the divide between the sharp blue of the sky and the crisp green of the trees could never be breached.

I parked and unfolded myself from the car like a calf finding her legs. I was awkward, and shaky, and wondered how my limbs would take my weight. With blinking eyes, a little blurry, I peered at the map. It was only about half a mile to the midpoint of a trail called the Lookout.

There weren't any other cars in the lot. I tucked my keys under the wheel and took off. My steps were heavy. I wasn't fast, but my body knew what to do. A few minutes in, I found my stride. My feet seemed to be in charge of the rhythm. I started running.

I had run before, for many years, but as a second thought. It was a way to stay in shape between excursions, keep my lungs strong when I was in the city, always an exercise in preparation for the real thing—paddling, climbing, skiing, or mountaineering. It was a way to counteract the hours I spent writing at my computer.

The trail was empty on the way up. My breath came hard. I kept thinking I heard something behind me. Around each corner, my eyes searched for something dark, twitching, darting, but there was nothing. Mostly it was the sound of my own breath bouncing off the rock. There was the smallest echo. I stopped, stood still, and listened. I was alone, but I kept looking to see if something else was there.

"The past is alive in the form of gnawing interior discomfort," Bessel van der Kolk writes in *The Body Keeps the Score*.

At the top of a trail, there is a large dome of granite. This is the lookout the trail gets its name from. I stood on the rock, puffing, trying to catch my breath. I put my palm to my heart to steady it. The sun rose and sharpened everything. The sky and the land seemed to touch each other. The granite perch overlooked hundreds of acres of the park. The trees rolled over lakes and dipped into valleys, as if each tree stood in a line that connected everything.

In the wake of the last ice age, the land was carved and bent as the ice shrunk back. I could imagine how it must have felt to stand in this same place a hundred years before. The rock would have been just as solid underfoot, and some of the same trees would have swayed in front of my eyes. The sky would have arced overhead regardless of its particular mood that day. Even ten thousand years ago, the changes would likely be slight; maybe the ridge to my left was more prominent, the lake deeper, a stand of trees thicker, and more old growth still in place.

The same idea could stretch forward. As long as the land remained protected, a person could stand in the same place I did. She could look out and see this view long after I was gone.

I cocked my ear in the direction of the woods. It was quiet. I could hear only the breeze and the sway of trees. Humans had shaped this place, and while knowing that, I could still love the landscape. There was no need to see it as untouched. And no dark shapes crashed out of the woods.

As I stood at the peak of the Lookout, there was danger. My instincts were correct about that, but it didn't come from the woods. If Algonquin Park is a place made by people, so were my ideas about cancer. I had an operation to cut out cancer with a margin around the diseased cells, as if a border might give me protection. It was tempting to put my fists up and say

I'd been unfairly targeted, but I knew that wasn't true. Cancer wasn't an attack. It was as much a part of me as the colour of my eyes, my sense of humour, or my blood type. Cancer is one in a long list of things my dad gave me.

There was nothing that would come crashing out of the woods, fangs bared, blood dripping. The danger came from a much more frightening place. Cancer would most likely attack me from the inside. My dad's death, the worst thing I could imagine, might be mine. And if I laid down my sword in Algonquin Park, if I didn't want to fight, that left me with two other responses: freeze or flight.

I started running more. As I did, the way I ran changed. It was no longer something I did to prepare or stay in shape. It became the main event.

Now I run most evenings. Sunscreen drips into my eyes as I follow alongside the edge of Lake Ontario. I've lived in Toronto for more than fifteen years since moving back. I grew up here, but when I was young, we thought of the lake as a place for industrial waste. Now there's a better understanding of the importance of the lake to the city's health. The shift in civic thinking is something I've internalized.

I leave the house two hours before sunset. During the darkest days in the winter, I go for my run as early as 2:41 p.m. In the spring in Toronto, the days grow longer by about a minute every day. Around the summer solstice, I wait until the shadows touch 7:03 p.m. before I leave the house.

"I don't believe in aging," wrote Virginia Woolf. "I believe in forever altering one's aspect to the sun."

I'm aware of the slightest changes in the light. The water looks and behaves in a new way every time I'm out. I don't think of it as going for a run, more like I go to see what the lake is saying on any given day. Sometimes I swear I can feel it breathing beside me. The water can be quiet and sly, like it's hiding something. On other days the lake is frantic, the headwinds furious. I follow along with its moods. There's so much beauty in a constant state of discovery.

In the winter, I run straight into the driving snow. It's as miserable as being high up on a mountain pass or on a long canoe trip, and every bit as spectacular. The winds on the shores of Lake Ontario are no less biting. With red cheeks, frozen eyelashes, and stiff fingers, I feel incredibly alive. By the time I struggle home, I'm sure I've been to the end of the earth and back.

One day, at the height of summer, it was too hot and humid. I came home dripping, exhausted, and announced I was quitting. The next day I woke up and heard the call of the lake. I'll keep going.

As I run, researchers are making advances in immunotherapy. In my case, cancer occurs because it gets around the immune system. Rather than raising a sword against the cancer cells, doctors are finding ways to enhance the body's natural defences. A cancer vaccine is one example. There's a trial under way for melanoma where a sample is taken of a tumour. A specialized vaccine can be designed, one that might help my CDKN2A gene to function, for example. Rather than destroying cells, as treatments have in the past, a vaccine helps train the immune system to identify the cancer cells and stop them from spreading. This kind of treatment is more than a technological advance. It's a shift in perspective. In my case, the disease comes from within. A cure might come from there too.

WILL I SURVIVE A bear attack? I'd been asking the wrong question. Being alive is one big risk and it will end in death, but the bridge between those two things is love.

After this investigation, my recommendation is to spend your time falling in love with the people and the world around you. Don't let a fear of death eclipse your life. Run toward love, fight for it, and die for it.

For many years, I remembered the last words my dad spoke to me in a certain way. I heard them as I did when I was nine years old. My experience of having cancer has allowed those words to grow. I understand them from a different perspective. It's a point of view that, given my age now, might be much closer to my dad's.

If I have to tell my sons that I'm dying, it will take incredible courage. And if I'm brave enough to express my fear, if I can be vulnerable and honest, the conversation might come with a sense of release. My boys are still young, but they have a loving family. I see their strength. I trust them. Life can be hard and, with love, they will find their own ways to weather it.

When Beowulf turns to face his final fight with the dragon, he knows he will die. In Maria Dahvana Headley's translation, he says, "I'll let go then, of all my holdings, my throne, my carefully guarded bones." It was acceptance that gave Beowulf the strength to be brave.

That's how I want to live. That's how I'll go.

NOTES

PART ONE: Fight for Your Life

1.

Draws from a trip to Bates Island, Opeongo Lake, Algonquin Park, with Jerry Schmanda on September 25, 2019.

Timeline also from interview with David and Cheryll Stott, August 2, 2019.

And from Dan Strickland, "What Can We Learn?," *The Best of the Raven* (Whitney, ON: The Friends of Algonquin Park, 1993).

David Euler and Mike Wilton, *Algonquin Park: The Human Impact* (Espanola, ON: Algonquin Eco Watch, 2009).

2.

Dale Brazao, "Bear Wouldn't Give Up Bodies of Campers," *Toronto Star*, October 18, 1991.

Claire Cameron, *The Bear* (New York: Little, Brown and Co.; Toronto: Doubleday, 2014).

For a discussion of the difficulties with reporting on attacks, see Eva Holland, "When a Fatal Grizzly Mauling Goes Viral," *Outside Magazine*, May 23, 2019.

The number of black bear attacks in North America, up to 2009, was sixty-three, as per Stephen Herrero, Andrew Higgins, James E. Cordoza, Laura I. Hajduk, and Tom S. Smith, "Fatal Attacks by

American Black Bear on People: 1900–2009," *Wildlife Management* 75, no. 3 (April 2011): 596–603.

Twenty-four people have been killed by a black bear in the last twenty years: Justin Hoffman and Alyssa Whoaa, "Fatal Black Bear Attacks in North America over the Last 20 Years," *Wide Open Spaces*, June 2023, www.wideopenspaces.com/black-bear-attacks-statistics/.

"List of Fatal bear attacks in North America," on Wikipedia, last checked on June 10, 2024, https://en.wikipedia.org/wiki/List_of_fatal_bear_attacks_in_North_America. Note that this list can be changed by an editor at any time. I did a spot check and have consulted experts who agree this list of fatalities, when it comes to wild black bears, seems fairly accurate.

Ideas about true crime and ethics were influenced by Mark O'Connell, *A Thread of Violence: A Story of Truth, Invention, and Murder* (Toronto: Doubleday, 2023), and Sarah Weinman, *Evidence of Things Seen: True Crime in an Era of Reckoning* (New York: Ecco, 2023).

L.P. Hartley, *The Go-Between* (London: Hamish Hamilton, 1953).

3.

Angus Cameron, linguist and lexicographer: https://en.wikipedia.org/wiki/Angus_Cameron_(academic).

The Dictionary of Old English: https://doe.artsci.utoronto.ca/.

Discussion of kennings in Old English draws from interview with Antoinette diPaolo Healey, the Angus Cameron Professor Emerita of Old English Studies, University of Toronto, October 9, 2019. Also from "Semantics and Vocabulary" by Dieter Kastovsky, in *The Cambridge History of the English Language, Vol. I: The Beginnings to 1066* by Richard M. Hogg (Cambridge: Cambridge University Press, 1992).

Chemotherapy from "Evolution of Cancer Treatments: Chemotherapy," American Cancer Society, June 12, 2014, www.cancer.org/cancer/cancer-basics/history-of-cancer/cancer-treatment-chemo.html.

Ideas about cancer and healing were influenced by Anne Boyer, *The Undying* (New York: Farrar, Straus and Giroux, 2019), and Susan Sontag, *Illness as Metaphor* (New York: Picador, 1977).

The translations of *Beowulf* I refer to the most: Maria Dahvana Headley, *Beowulf: A New Translation* (New York: Farrar, Straus and Giroux, 2020), and Seamus Heaney, *Beowulf: A New Verse Translation Bilingual Edition* (New York: W.W. Norton, 2001).

PART TWO: Be Prepared

4.

"Algonquin Park Canoe Routes," available on the official website of the Friends of Algonquin Park. I referred to the 2012–13 edition while writing.

From the author's memories of two canoe trips led for Camp Wapomeo, Algonquin Park, Ontario, July–August 1992.

Brazao, "Bear Wouldn't Give Up."

John Duncanson, "Couple Enjoyed Camping in Park," *Toronto Star*, October 18, 1991.

5.

The street where Raymond Jakubauskas lived was identified in a newspaper article.

Statistics Canada, Census of Population, www12.statcan.gc.ca/census-recensement/index-eng.cfm.

John Duncanson, "Algonquin Park Was a Retreat for a Couple Who Loved to Camp," *Toronto Star*, October 18, 1991.

Information from an email sent by Regan Martin in 2014 used with permission.

Graeme Wynn, "Behind the Canadian Shield," *Canadian Geographic*, May 10, 2019.

History of Algonquin Park draws from Algonquin Logging Museum exhibits, Algonquin Park, Whitney, ON.

"The King's Highway 60," website maintained by Cameron Bevers, 2002–19, www.thekingshighway.ca/Highway60.htm.

Bernard S. Shaw, *Lake Opeongo: Untold Stories of Algonquin Park's Largest Lake* (Burnstown, ON: General Store Publishing House, 1998).

Algonquin Park facts from Archived Backgrounder, Government of Ontario, November 2, 2009, news.ontario.ca/mnr/en/2009/11/algonquin-provincial-park.html.

On the water at 5:30 p.m., detail from Andrew Dreschel, "Campers' Deaths," *Vancouver Sun*, October 30, 1991.

6.

Dave Taylor, *Black Bears: A Natural History* (Markham, ON: Fitzhenry & Whiteside, 2021).

Gloria Dickie, *Eight Bears: Mythic Past and Imperiled Future* (New York: W.W. Norton, 2023).

"Do Bears Actually Hibernate?," *Science World*, February 19, 2016.

"World's oldest-known wild black bear dies at 39," Bear With Us, August 27, 2013, https://bearwithus.org/the-oldest-known-wild-bear-dies-at-39-5-years-old-she-would-have-been-40-years-old-january-2014/.

Balsam branch inspired by a phone conversation with biologist Mike Wilton on August 2, 2019. He observed a bear taking a branch into a den, which seemed unique behaviour to this particular bear.

Seasonal patterns of black bears in Algonquin from interview with Jeremy Inglis, August 31, 2019.

Jeremy E. Inglis and Mike L. Wilton, "Seasonal Movements, Patterns and Feeding Habits of Large Adult Black Bears in Algonquin Park Ontario," *Ontario Ministry of National Resources, Parks and Protected Areas Research in Ontario*, 1998.

"345kg bear shot in Longlac rivals Ontario record," CBC News, September 26, 2014.

Dan Strickland and Russell J. Rutter, *Mammals of Algonquin Provincial Park* (Ontario: Ministry of Natural Resources, 1978).

Necropsy report filed by Dr. Ian K. Barker, October 21, 1991. Occurrence report filed by Ontario Provincial Police, October 15, 1991, and "Supplementary Report. Briefing Note, Subject: Bear Attack in Algonquin Provincial," date redacted. All were obtained through the Freedom of Information and Protection of Privacy Act.

Troy I. Raglus, Bert De Groef, Simone Rochfort, Grant Rawlin, and Christina McCown, "Bone Marrow Fat Analysis as a Diagnostic

Tool to Document Ante-mortem Starvation," *Veterinary Journal* 243 (January 2019): 1–7.

PART THREE: Secure Your Food

7.

Ideas about fear were influenced by Daniel Gardner, *The Science of Fear: Why We Fear the Things We Shouldn't—and Put Ourselves in Greater Danger* (New York: Dutton, 2008), and Eva Holland, *Nerve: A Personal Journey through the Science of Fear* (Toronto: Penguin Random House, 2021).

From the author's memories of tree planting with Outland Reforestation in 1993 and A&M Reforestation in 1994 in the bush near Hearst, Ontario.

For a discussion of bear relocation at that time: Jeremy E. Inglis, "An Analysis of Human–Black Bear Conflicts in Algonquin Provincial Park, Ontario (1973–1990)," Ministry of Natural Resources, in Proceedings: 11th Eastern Black Bear Workshop.

8.

Sunrise and sunset times in Algonquin Park: sunrise.maplogs.com/algonquin_park_on_poa_canada.91139.html.

W.H. Auden, "First Things First," *New Yorker*, March 1, 1957.

The chapter compiles the author's memories and sources, including interviews with Jerry Schmanda and David Stott, second-hand accounts, newspaper articles, and a visit to Bates Island in the 1990s.

On the water at 5:30 p.m. from Dreschel, "Campers' Deaths."

Stephen Herrero, *Bear Attacks: Their Causes and Avoidance*, 3rd ed. (Lanham, MD: Lyons Press, 2018).

9.

Seasonal patterns of black bears in Algonquin from interview with Jeremy Inglis, August 31, 2019.

Inglis and Wilton, "Seasonal Movements."

L.L. Rogers, P.S. Beringer, D.A. Trauba, and G.A. Wilker, "Fawn Predation by Black Bears in Northeastern Minnesota" (Ely, MN: North Central Experiment Station, undated report).

L.L. Rogers, G.A. Wilker, and S.S. Scott, "What Is Important to Black Bears in the Lakes States," Duluth, MN: Aspen Symposium, July 25–27, 1989.

Taylor, *Black Bears.*

Dickie, *Eight Bears.*

A note about staring into the eyes of a bear that I've forced myself to move to the notes: In *Grizzly Man* (Lionsgate, 2005), a documentary, Werner Herzog narrates a similar moment. The film was assembled with footage from the close-up camera of a grizzly bear enthusiast named Timothy Treadwell, who had a misplaced kinship with wild brown bears in Alaska. When commenting on a grizzly bear who makes eye contact with a camera, Herzog tells us what he sees. "I discover no kinship, no understanding, no mercy. I see only the overwhelming indifference of nature. To me, there is no such thing as a secret world of the bears. And this blank stare speaks only of a half-bored interest in food." But the grizzly Herzog described was lounging in a meadow. The black bear, as he looked at Tom's camera, was stalking. I see intelligence.

Pam Belluck, "Study of Black Bears Finds It's Not the Mamas That Should Be Feared the Most," *New York Times*, May 11, 2011.

Tom Walter's footage and interview appear in *Bear Attack Trilogy Part 1: Bear Attack: The Predatory Black Bear*, an Ellis Vision Production in association with CFCN-TV Calgary and the Discovery Channel Canada, 1999.

PART FOUR: Keep Your Distance

10.

Glacier on Mt. Hood, Oregon, 1995. Climbing trip to Joshua Tree in 1996.

Family trip to Algonquin Park, 2013.

Andrew Skurka, "How to Protect Food from Bears," *Outside Magazine*, January 26, 2019.

Lisa Richardson told me the story about the bear in Quebec, retold from memory.

Personal notebooks, undated.

Section draws from excursion to Bates Island, Opeongo Lake, Algonquin Park with Jerry Schmanda on September 25, 2019, and from interview with David and Cheryll Stott, August 2, 2019.

11.

Herrero, *Bear Attacks*.

"Know the Difference," Bear Smart Society, www.bearsmart.com/about-bears/know-the-difference/.

Bryce Andrews, *Down from the Mountain: The Life and Death of a Grizzly Bear* (New York: Houghton Mifflin Harcourt, 2019).

Taylor, *Black Bears*.

"Backgrounder on Black Bears in Ontario," Ontario Ministry of Natural Resources, June 2009.

Barrie K. Gilbert, *One of Us: A Biologist's Walk among Bears* (Victoria: FriesenPress, 2019).

Dickie, *Eight Bears*.

United National Office on Drugs and Crime, "Killings of Women and Girls by Their Intimate Partner or Other Family Members: Global Estimates 2020," November 2021.

Erica Berry, *Wolfish: Wolf, Self, and the Stories We Tell about Fear* (New York: Flatiron Books, 2023). This book is superb, one of the best on women's life experiences, the wild, and fear: "Women, like wolves, have long been faulted, not only for crossing the boundaries made by others, but for lacking boundaries themselves."

Olga Khazan, "Nearly Half of All Murdered Women Are Killed by Romantic Partners," *Atlantic*, July 20, 2017; Anne Kingston, "We Are the Dead," *Maclean's*, September 17, 2019.

"National Estimates of Outdoor Recreational Injuries Treated in Emergency Departments, United States, 2004–2005," Division of Unintentional Injury Prevention, National Center for Injury Prevention and Control, Centers for Disease Control and Prevention. Also Mike Rogers, "Bear Attacks—Killer Statistic That May Surprise You," *Alaska Life*, July 2017.

Conversation with Rick Stronks, Chief Park Naturalist, Algonquin Park, August 2, 2019.

Email from Regan Martin.

Bear spray was developed by Carrie Hunt, a biologist at the University of Montana, in the 1980s. After finding some bear deterrent potential in personal and military-grade pepper spray, she worked on the formula. It's a chemical irritant that is more potent than pepper spray. Bear spray has six times the amount of spray and is under more pressure compared with pepper spray. It is designed to deploy in a cone-shaped cloud. Capsaicin is the active ingredient. The recommendation from Hunt's study is to spray for seven seconds when the bear is thirty feet in front of you.

Stephen Herrero and Andrew Higgins, "Field Use of Capsicum Spray as a Bear Deterrent," University of Calgary, January 1998.

"Photographer Uses Bear Spray during Encounter on Wakesiu Lake Trail," Global News, June 9, 2022, globalnews.ca/video/8910203/photographer-encouters-bear-on-wakesiu-lake-trail.

Carrie Hunt, "Vol. 1, Behavioral Responses of Bears to Test of Repellents, Deterrents and Aversive Conditions," University of Montana, 1984.

Tom S. Smith, Stephen Herrero, Terry D. Debruyn, and James M. Wilder, "Efficacy of Bear Deterrent Spray in Alaska," *Journal of Wildlife Management* 72, no. 3 (December 2010): 640–45; *Wild Ontario* with James Alofs (podcast), Episode 6, "Curtis Matwishyn: How I Survived a Black Bear Attack."

Crystal Atamian, "Bear Spray Science," *Out There Outdoors*, August 18, 2002.

"Spray More Effective than Guns against Bears: Study," CBC News, March 26, 2008.

"Hunter in Grizzly Bear Attack Was Killed by a Gunshot from His Friend," *Daily Mail*, September 24, 2011.

"Spray Does the Trick for Photographer Pursued by Bear," *Storyful News & Weather*, posted on June 6, 2022.

Interview with Jeremy Inglis, August 31, 2019, Pembroke, Ontario.

Interview with Mike Wilton, August 2, 2019.

Strickland, "What Can We Learn?"

12.

Mark Kaufman, "The Fat Bears Sense the World in an Extraordinary Way," *Mashable*, October 9, 2022.

Ed Yong, *An Immense World: How Animal Senses Reveal the Hidden Realms Around Us* (Toronto: Alfred A. Knopf Canada, 2022).

"Meet the Black Bear," Bearwise.org, bearwise.org/all-about-black-bears/.

"Courtship and Mating," North American Bear Center, founded by Dr. Lynn Rogers, Ely, MN.

"Reproduction," Bear Smart Society, bearsmart.com/about-bears /reproduction/.

Inglis and Wilton, "Seasonal Movements."

Yasmin Tayag, "Scientists Learn Why Some Animals (But Not Humans) Still Have a Penis Bone," *Inverse*, September 18, 2018.

Preston A. Taylor, Maximilian L. Allen, and Micaela S. Gunter, "Black Bear Marking Behaviour at Rub Trees during the Breeding Season in Northern California," *Behaviour*, May 2015.

"Black Bear Safety," official website of the Friends of Algonquin Park, www.algonquinpark.on.ca/visit/recreational_activites/black-bear-safety-rules.php.

Frans De Waal, *Are We Smart Enough to Know How Smart Animals Are?* (New York: W.W. Norton, 2016).

Benjamin Kilham, *Out on a Limb: What Black Bears Have Taught Me about Intelligence and Intuition* (White River Junction, VT: Chelsea Green Publishing, 2013).

Dickie, *Eight Bears*.

PART FIVE: Close Encounters

13.

Memories from family road trip, 2018.

Test results and author's appointment with Dr. Toubassi, November 12, 2018.

"Semantics and Vocabulary" by Dieter Kastovsky, in *The Cambridge History of the English Language, Vol. I: The Beginnings to 1066* by Richard M. Hogg (Cambridge: Cambridge University Press, 1992).

14.

Christine Sismondo, "The Odd, Complicated History of Canadian Thanksgiving," *Maclean's*, October 5, 2017.

"Briefing Note, Subject: Bear Attack in Algonquin Provincial," date redacted, obtained through a filing under the Freedom of Information and Protection of Privacy Act.

Duncanson, "Couple Enjoyed Camping in Park."

Dreschel, "Campers' Deaths."

Other details: Brazao, "Bear Wouldn't Give Up"; "Algonquin Park Was Retreat for Couple Who Loved to Camp," *Toronto Star*, October 18, 1991; Marline Parks, "Campers Killed by Black Bear," *Bancroft Times*, October 22, 1991; Patricia McLee, "Black Bear Kills Campers in Algonquin," *Barry's Bay This Week*, October 22, 1991; Ray Stamplecoski, "Bear Attack Kills Two Park Campers," *Eganville Leader*, October 23, 1991; Canadian Press, "Kill Bear Kept Campers for Food," *Gazette* (Montreal), October 19, 1991; Ian MacLeod, "Bear Attack: Killing of Campers Astonishes Park Officials," *Ottawa Citizen*, October 18, 1991; Mark Stewart, "Black Bear Kills Couple," *Toronto Sun*, October 17, 1991; Andrew Dreschel, "Pair Died of Head Blows, Police Who Killed Bear Say," *Vancouver Sun*, October 30, 1991.

Section also draws from interview with Jerry Schmanda, September 25, 2019, and interview with David Stott, August 2, 2019.

15.

Stephen Herrero, "Social Behaviour of Black Bears at a Garbage Dump in Jasper National Park," *Bears: Their Biology and Management* 5 (January 1983).

Phone conversation with Stephen Herrero and Linda Wiggins, September 24, 2019.

Kilham, *Out on a Limb*.

Jennifer Vonk and Michael J. Beran, "Bears 'Count' Too: Quantity Estimation and Comparison in Black Bears, *Ursus Americanus*," *Animal Behaviour* 84, no. 1 (July 2012): 231–38.

Rebecca McPhee, "Why Bears Are Even Smarter Than We Thought," *Explorersweb*, May 5, 2023.

Dickie, *Eight Bears.*
Taylor, *Black Bears.*
Inglis and Wilton, "Seasonal Movements."
My ideas about animal consciousness are influenced by De Waal, *Are We Smart Enough*; Charles Foster, *Being a Beast: Adventures across the Species Divide* (New York: Henry Holt, 2016); Barbara Gowdy, *The White Bone* (Toronto: Harper Perennial, 2007); Ed Yong, *An Immense World: How Animal Senses Reveal the Hidden Realms around Us* (Toronto: Alfred A. Knopf Canada, 2022); and Kristin Andrews, *The Animal Mind: An Introduction to the Philosophy of Animal Cognition*, 2nd ed. (London: Routledge, 2020).
About loner bears: "Bears," *National Geographic*, website accessed on December 19, 2019; "Black Bear," National Wildlife Federation, website accessed on December 19, 2019; "About Black Bears," *Mass Audubon*, website accessed on December 19, 2019.
Interview with Jeremy Inglis, July 31, 2019, Pembroke, Ontario.
Interview with Mike Wilton, August 2, 2019.

PART SIX: Defence vs. Offence

16.
Claire Cameron, *The Bear* (Toronto: Doubleday, 2014).
Genetic test results, March 2019.
Consultation with Emily Thain, Genetic Counsellor, Familial Cancer Clinic, Princess Margaret Cancer Centre, Toronto, with additional consultation from Dr. Raymond Kim and Dr. Wei Xu.
Candace D. Middlebrooks, Mark L. Stacey, Qing Li, Carrie Snyder, Trudy G. Shaw, Tami Richardson-Nelson, Marc Rendell, et al., "Analysis of the CDKN2A Gene in FAMMM Syndrome Families Reveals Early Age Onset for Additional Symdromic Cancers," American Association for Cancer Research, June 26, 2019.
Meeting with Dr. Michael Reedjik, March 2019.
Brazao, "Bear Wouldn't Give Up."

PART SEVEN: Finding a Cache

17.

Photo of bear is credited to Senior Constable Wayne McCarvey of the Perth detachment, Ontario Provincial Police, and appears in Gord Murray, "Bear Attack Not Expected to Cut Algonquin Crowd," unidentified local newspaper, November 8, 1991.

Interview with Jeremy Inglis, July 31, 2019, Pembroke, Ontario.

Interview with Mike Wilton, August 2, 2019.

Observations made alongside Phoebe Cameron, golden retriever, on October 10, 2019.

Kilham, *Out on a Limb.*

Toni Morrison, "Grendel and His Mother," in *The Source of Self-Regard* (New York: Penguin Random House, 2019).

18.

Section draws from interview with Jerry Schmanda, September 25, 2019, and interview with David and Cheryll Stott, August 2, 2019.

Conversation with Rick Stronks, Chief Park Naturalist, Algonquin Park, August 2, 2019.

Additional details from sources listed in chapter 14.

Lauren Groff, *Fates and Furies* (New York: Riverhead, 2015).

Foster, *Being a Beast.*

19.

"Black bear and coyote caught on video hanging out," www.youtube.com/watch?v=IU05ob0b5D4.

Philip Kiefer, "Gray Foxes Use Black Bears as Personal Body Guards," *Popular Science*, June 7, 2021.

Maximilian L. Allen, Heiko U. Wittmer, Akino Ingaki, Koji Yamazaki, and Shinsuke Koike, "Food Caching by Bears: A Literature Review and New Observations for Asiatic and American Black Bears," *Ursus* 2021, no. 32 (January 2021): 32e10.

Luis Alberto Urrea, *The Devil's Highway: A True Story* (New York: Back Bay Books, 2005).

PART EIGHT: When to Play Dead

20.

Balmoral Hotel, Barry's Bay, ON, August 1, 2019.

History of Algonquin Park draws from Algonquin Logging Museum exhibits, Algonquin Park, Whitney, ON.

Paul F.J. Eagles and Grace A.A. Bandoh, "Visitor and Tourism Management in Algonquin Provincial Park: The Past, Present and Future," in *Algonquin Park: The Human Impact*, ed. David Euler and Mike Wilton (Spring Bay, ON: Algonquin Eco Watch, 2009).

Chief Kirby Whiteduck, "Our Majestic Forests: An Aboriginal View of Algonquin Park," in *Algonquin Park: The Human Impact*, ed. David Euler and Mike Wilton (Spring Bay, ON: Algonquin Eco Watch, 2009).

Trish Manning, "Spend a Day in Algonquin Park Exploring the Life, Art and Death of Tom Thomson," *Northern Ontario Travel*, April 27, 2018.

Richard Grant, "The Lost History of Yellowstone: Debunking the Myth That the Great National Park Was a Wilderness Untouched by Humans," *Smithsonian Magazine*, January 2021.

Robert Jago, "Canada's National Parks Are Colonial Crime Scenes," *Walrus*, June 10, 2020.

My thinking about myths in Canadian history is influenced by Michelle Good, *Truth Telling: Seven Conversations about Indigenous Life in Canada* (Toronto: HarperCollins Canada, 2023).

21.

Section draws from interview with Jerry Schmanda, September 25, 2019, and interview with David and Cheryll Stott, August 2, 2019.

Additional details from sources listed in chapter 14.

"Bear Encounter," Yellowstone National Park Service, www.nps.gov/yell/learn/nature/bearreact.htm.

"Staying Safe in Bear Country: Bear Spray & Firearms," National Park Service, March 23, 2022, https://www.nps.gov/articles/bearsprayfirearms.htm.

Radiant Lake timeline and story established from newspaper articles (without bylines) including: "Fatal Bear Attack First in 100 Years," *Ottawa Citizen*, May 16, 1978; "Autopsies Set on Three Boys Killed by Bear," *Ottawa Citizen*, May 16, 1978; "300-Pound Bear Thought to Be Boys' Killer," *Calgary Herald*, May 17, 1978; "Fish in Jacket Believed behind Grisly Deaths," *Ottawa Citizen*, May 17, 1978; "Youths May Not Have Heard Killer Bear Approaching," *Ottawa Journal*, May 17, 1978; "Autopsies Confirm Youths Mauled to Death by Bear," *Red Deer Advocate*, May 18, 1978; and "Bear Tragedy Termed Case of Mistaken Identity," *Ottawa Citizen*, July 12, 1978. Details also appear in the following books: Herrero, *Bear Attacks*, pp. 113–16, and Mike Cramond, *Killer Bears* (Lanham, MD: Lyons Press, 1981), pp. 60–81.

Belluck, "Study of Black Bears."

Herrero et al., "Fatal Attacks by American Black Bear."

"Bear-Inflicted Human Injuries in Yellowstone National Park, 1970–1994," *Ursus*, International Association for Bear Research and Management, Vol. 10, pp. 377–84.

Wayne David, "A Casual Theory of Experiential Fear," *Canadian Journal of Philosophy* 18, no. 3 (September 1988): 459–83.

22.

Necropsy report filed by Dr. Ian K. Barker, October 21, 1991. Occurrence report filed by Ontario Provincial Police, October 15, 1991, and "Supplementary Report. Briefing Note, Subject: Bear Attack in Algonquin Provincial," date redacted. All were obtained through the Freedom of Information and Protection of Privacy Act.

"Bearwise: Bear Safety Tips for Hunters." www.bearwise.org/bear-safety-tips/hunting-safety/.

Bird feeder intel in podcast interview for the Ministry of National Resources and Forestry with Jeremy Inglis, September 27, 2023.

Number of black bears hunted in Canada: The data is collected by province, so I made an estimate. Some advocacy groups double the number, as much as forty thousand.

Inglis and Wilton, "Seasonal Movements."

My estimate of black bears legally hunted yearly in Canada is based on a calculation of provincial numbers. North American numbers from Canadian Wildlife Federation, www.hww.ca/en/wildlife/mammals/black-bear.html.

Radiant Lake sources from chapter 20.

PART NINE: How to Be Brave

23.

Ideas in this chapter influenced by Bessel van der Kolk, *The Body Keeps the Score: Brain, Mind, and Body in the Healing of Trauma* (Pub City: Penguin, 2015), and, especially, conversations with Sara Peters, registered psychotherapist.

Doctor appointment with Dr. Toubassi, June 2019.

Naomi Wilcox, Martine Dumont, Anna González-Neira, et al., "Exome Sequencing Identifies Breast Cancer Susceptibility Genes and Defines the Contribution of Coding Variants to Breast Cancer Risk," *Nature Genetics* 55, no. 9 (September 2023): 1435–39.

Eye surgery, Princess Margaret Hospital, Toronto, October 2020.

Conversation with Ben and Max Cameron, June 2021.

Headley, *Beowulf.*

"Beowulf: The Monsters and the Critics," a 1936 lecture given by J.R.R. Tolkien.

Stephen T. Asma, "Monsters on the Brain: An Evolutionary Epistemology of Horror," *Social Research* 81, no. 4 (Winter 2014): 941–68.

24.

Necropsy report filed by Dr. Ian K. Barker, October 21, 1991.

Occurrence report filed by Ontario Provincial Police, October 15, 1991, and "Supplementary Report. Briefing Note, Subject: Bear Attack in Algonquin Provincial," date redacted. All were obtained through the Freedom of Information and Protection of Privacy Act.

Section draws from excursion to Bates Island, Opeongo Lake, Algonquin Park, with Jerry Schmanda on September 25, 2019, and from interview with David and Cheryll Stott, August 2, 2019.

Occurrence report filed by Ontario Provincial Police, October 15, 1991, and undated supplementary report.

"Comparison of Weight of Opeongo 'Killer Bear' with Weights of Large Bears Trapped by George Kolensky and Staff in North Bay District," *MNR Research*, October 25, 1991.

Seasonal patterns of black bears in Algonquin from interview with Jeremy Inglis, August 31, 2019.

Inglis and Wilton, "Seasonal Movements."

"Feeding Sign," North American Bear Center, Ely, MN, https://bear.org/feeding-sign/.

25.

"5 Stages of Activity and Hibernation," North American Bear Center, Ely, MN, https://bear.org/5-stage-of-activity-and-hibernation.

Seasonal patterns of black bears in Algonquin from interview with Jeremy Inglis, August 31, 2019.

Taylor, *Black Bears*.

PART TEN: When to Fight

26.

Based on overnight trip with David Cameron to Bates Island, Opeongo Lake, Algonquin Park, October 11, 2019.

Strickland, "What Can We Learn?"

Heaney, *Beowulf*.

27.

Draws on many of the same sources as chapter 24.

Herrero, *Bear Attacks*.

Interview with Laura Darby on August 21, 2023.

Heather Latter, "Woman Shares Harrowing Bear Attack Story," *Fort Frances Times*, January 9, 2013.

John Geiger, *The Third Man Factor: The Secret to Survival in Extreme Environments* (Toronto: Penguin Canada, 2009).

Joe Simpson, *Touching the Void* (London: Vintage, 1988).

Tad Friend, "Jumpers: The Fatal Grandeur of the Golden Gate Bridge," *New Yorker*, October 5, 2003.

28.

Draws on the same sources as chapter 24 and email interview with Chuck Fisher, July 23, 2023, with permission.

PART ELEVEN: A Time to Surrender

29.

Based on overnight trip with David Cameron to Bates Island, Opeongo Lake, Algonquin Park, October 11, 2019.

Herrero, *Bear Attacks*.

Necropsy report filed by Dr. Ian K. Barker, October 21, 1991.

Draws on the sources from chapter 24.

Heaney, *Beowulf*.

30.

My ideas about animal consciousness are drawn from sources listed in chapter 15.

Bill Mayer, "Does a Bear Think in the Woods," *Sierra Club*, September 19, 2019.

Raglus et al., "Bone Marrow Fat Analysis."

31.

Draws on sources in the previous two chapters.

PART TWELVE: How to Live

32.

Ellen Vanstone, "Bad News Bears," *Globe and Mail*, October 10, 1992.

Herrero et al., "Fatal Attacks by American Black Bear."

Mike Commito, "Every Bear Attack One Too Many," letter to the editor, *Northern Life*, August 1, 2012.

Emails from Regan Martin and Sven Frehe, with permission.

33.

Zoom call with Laura Darby, August 21, 2023.

M.E. Obbard, E.J. Newton, D. Potter, A. Orton, B.R. Patterson, and B.D. Steinberg, "Big Enough for Bears? American Black Bears at Heightened Risk of Mortality during Seasonal Forays outside Algonquin Provincial Park, Ontario," *Ursus* 28, no. 2 (November 2017): 182–94.

For a discussion of road ecology, see Ben Goldfarb, "How Cars Ruin Wild Animals' Lives," *Vox*, September 12, 2023.

Taylor, *Black Bears*.

Jon P. Beckman and Carl W. Lackey, "Lessons Learned from a 20-Year Collaborative Study on American Black Bears," *Human–Wildlife Interactions* 12, no. 3 (December 2018): 396–404.

Black bears have been known to travel up to sixty miles for a seasonal feast. A study of black bears living near the towns in the Lake Tahoe area of California found that, given easy access to human food sources, bears contracted their ranges; they moved between 70 and 90 percent less. As Jeremy Inglis said, "The drive is huge to put on enough weight . . . they will take chances."

Herrero et al., "Fatal Attacks by American Black Bear."

"List of Fatal bear attacks in North America," on Wikipedia.

R. Eliot Crafton, Laura B. Comay, and Marc Humphries, "Oil and Gas Activities within the National Wildlife Refuge System," Congressional Research Service, May 9, 2018, https://sgp.fas.org/crs/misc/R45192.pdf.

Sarah Fecht, "Arctic National Wildlife Refuge: How Drilling for Oil

Could Impact Wildlife," *State of the Planet*, December 6, 2017, https://news.climate.columbia.edu/2017/12/06/arctic-national-wildlife-refuge-drilling-oil-impact-wildlife/.

Clark Mindock, "Yellowstone Area Logging Approvals Challenged over Grizzly Bear, Climate Impacts," Reuters, September 21, 2023.

Louise Cullen, "Ireland Could Give Nature Constitutional Rights," BBC, December 16, 2013.

Eleanor Roy and Roy Ainge, "New Zealand River Granted Same Legal Rights as Human Beings," *Guardian*, March 16, 2017.

Chloe Berge, "This Canadian River Is Now Legally a Person. It's Not the Only One," *National Geographic*, April 15, 2022.

Elizabeth Benner, "This Pristine Canadian River Has Legal Personhood, a New Approach to Conserving Nature," CBC, February 1, 2024.

Logging Algonquin: The Fight for the Forest Never Rests, documentary film by Conor Devries, 2023.

Benjy Radcliffe, "The Corporation as a Person: Legal Fact or Fiction?" TheCourt.ca, September 24, 2009.

Nina Totenberg, "When Did Companies Become People? Excavating the Legal Evolution," NPR, July 28, 2014.

Sarah Cox, "Old-Growth Logging Leaves Black Bears without Dens: Biologist," *Narwhal*, May 27, 2019.

Cancer information from the American Society of Clinical Oncology–run website, Cancer.net, www.cancer.net/navigating-cancer-care/how-cancer-treated/immunotherapy-and-vaccines/what-are-cancer-vaccines.

34.

Lookout run, Algonquin Park, August 2, 2019.

For links, information and resources about staying safe in bear country, please visit www.claire-cameron.com.

ACKNOWLEDGEMENTS

I AM INCREDIBLY FORTUNATE to work with my longtime editor, Kiara Kent—I can't wait for our next adventure. A special thank you to my agent, Richard Pine, for his unwavering belief in this book, and also to Naomi Eisenbeiss and Eliza Rothstein at InkWell Management. I'm grateful to the team at Penguin Random House Canada for their continued support, including Amy Black, Susan Burns, Kristin Cochrane, Emma Dolan, Ashley Dunn, Martha Kanya-Forstner, Christie Hanson, Sharon Klein, Martha Leonard, copyeditor John Sweet, proofreader Sue Sumeraj, and the audiobook team, Zak Annette, Rachel Cairns, and Sonia Vaillant.

To my friends, editors, and early readers, our conversations have added so much to this book: Jami Attenberg, Jim Bull, Claudia Dey, Omar El Akkad, Amy Fisher, Hannah Gersen, Leigh-Anne Graham, Jonathan Howland, Erin Mulligan, Sarah Murphy, Lindsay Oughtred, Jackie Pye, Dustin Schell, Emily Sewell, Sophie Wright Sinclair, Heidi Sopinka, and Miriam Toews.

Thank you to all who were incredibly generous with their time, expertise, and trust, especially Laura Darby, Chuck Fisher,

Sven Frehe, Stephen Herrero and Linda Wiggins, Jeremy Inglis, Regan Martin, Sara Peters, Jerry Schmanda, David and Cheryll Stott, Rick Stronks, and Mike Wilton.

Thank you to Dr. Philip Doiron, Dr. Michael Reedijk, Dr. Diana Toubassi and The Toronto Western Family Health Team for your kindness, expertise, and care.

Sections of Chapters 3 and 34 were first published in *The Globe and Mail* on July 29, 2023, in the article "After I was diagnosed with the same type of skin cancer that killed my father, I had to alter my relationship with the sun." Sections of chapter 7 were first published in *The New York Times* on September 15, 2023, in the article "We Thought We Were Saving the Planet, but We Were Planting a Time Bomb." Sections of chapter 29 were first mentioned in *Outside* magazine on May 19, 2024, in the article "How a Skin Cancer Diagnosis Changed My Relationship with the Outdoors."

I appreciate the support of the Canada Council for the Arts, who provided me with the time and space to write.

A final thank you to my family, who have loved me through it all: Ben, Dave, Ian and Bev, Max, Phoebe, Susannah, and Wendy Cameron.

© Trish Mennell

CLAIRE CAMERON's most recent novel, *The Last Neanderthal*, was a national bestseller and a finalist for the 2017 Rogers Writers' Trust Fiction Prize. It sold in eleven territories. Her second novel, *The Bear*, was longlisted for the Women's Prize for Fiction, sold in ten territories, and was a #1 national bestseller. It won the Northern Lit Award from the Ontario Library Service, which her first novel, *The Line Painter*, also won. Claire has led canoe trips in Algonquin Park and worked as an instructor for Outward Bound, teaching mountaineering, climbing, and whitewater rafting in Oregon and beyond. Her writing has appeared in *The New Yorker*, *The New York Times*, and *The Guardian*, and she is a monthly contributor to *The Globe and Mail*. She lives in Toronto.